BERNADETTE PETERS HATES ME:

TRUE TALES FROM A

DELUSIONAL MAN

BY

KEITH A. STEWART

Cover design by Dwayne Booth. Book design by HumorOutcasts Press.

Published 2016 by HumorOutcasts Press
Printed in the United States of America

ISBN: 0-692-65995-1
EAN-13: 978-069265995-3

For Andy, Mom, and anyone else I have embarrassed along the way.

Contents

Introduction

Hi there!

Welcome to the book. Before you dive into all the craziness, I just want to give you a heads up—this book is intended to be funny. It is not meant to be the next great work of American literature, but if it somehow turns in to that, then so be it. I hope you are ready to laugh, shake your head, and say, "Oh, Keith!" Because that's going to happen. I bet. Well, it might not, but it could. If it does, will you please take a selfie of yourself doing it and tweet it to me? @Shiglyogly

All the stories are true, and happened to yours truly. I have changed the names of a few people and places to save them from potential embarrassment (and myself from attorney fees and court costs). If you have been on an actual adventure with me that has made this book, and while reading it, you discover I've written about you in a way that makes you look like a real boob, and on top of that, used your real name in the story, then odds are you should have been nicer to me at some point. In particular, while I was writing this. It's your own fault, really.

I often say I have a Dark Cloud that follows me around causing bad luck and mayhem wherever I go. This Dark Cloud is the root and fertilizer for nearly all my stories. My own mother tells me it takes a strong man to live my life, which is how I got the name for my blog, www.astrongmanscupoftea.com. But honestly, I don't believe my luck is any worse than anyone else's. I just choose to tell the stories of the unflattering and humiliating things that happen to me on a day-to-day basis. I think people relate to the stories because the same things happen to them. They just have never stopped to think for a minute that the situation was funny and not mortifying. So, maybe you will see yourself in a story or two as you read along.

If you do, I hope you can laugh extra hard, and remember that it wasn't so bad after all.

A writing mentor of mine at the Appalachian Writers Conference told me to make sure there was a universal truth in everything I wrote. I struggled with this for a while, trying to overthink each essay and make them unnecessarily "deep," many times altogether losing the humor in the piece. I finally realized that humor itself is a universal truth. Everyone needs to laugh and feel good. Everyone needs something to pick them up and give them a moment or two of pleasure. That is my intent for this book. I hope it brightens your day as much as you have brightened mine for taking the time to read it.

Now, go have some fun! And by go have some fun, I mean turn the page and start reading the book, not put the book down and go have a party or do something else. OK? OK. Go.

Song of Bernadette

Bernadette Peters hates me. No sugar coating can be applied to make that statement any less harsh or less true. It's a fact of which I am not particularly proud, but then I would hope neither is Bernadette. After all, as in most friendship-ending arguments, both sides usually say and do things they later regret. I am willing to forgive and forget, but Bernadette has yet to extend an olive branch with her dainty, sweet smelling, perfectly manicured hand. I suppose I could be the bigger person and offer her the branch with my freakishly similar—yet not as sweet smelling or manicured—dainty hand, but I am unsure of the expiration date, if any, on restraining orders issued from the city of Cincinnati police department. When Ms. Peters is angry she plays hard ball, and as you would expect from most divas, she is very unforgiving.

Broadway prima donnas and their show tunes have always been two of my great loves. As early as age five, I created my own diva persona, Rosie Red. I transformed into Rosie when the urge to perform on the stage overwhelmed my normal needs of playing kickball with my sister or building yet another cabin with my set of Lincoln Logs. All I had to do in order to call Rosie Red to me was wrap a bath towel around my head to imitate hair.

The color of the towel did not have to be red. We never had anything as impractical as red towels in our home. My mother was a staunch believer in the power of liquid bleach, and white was the only color that could withstand her heavy-handed pouring on laundry day. No, the red in Rosie Red was a figurative term. It was the attitude and sass that Rosie exuded, and as a five year old, the only way I knew to describe it was with color, and that color was red.

The wrapping of the towel around my head was also crucial to Rosie Red's identity. It was not wrapped into a cone-shaped pile like my mother and older sister fixed after they washed their hair. I draped the towel over my head, much like a boy performing the role of Shepherd Number One in his church's Christmas nativity play. I would then crease a small fold above my eyebrows that would help frame my face and give an appearance of bangs and texture. The cascade of the towel would create enough length and body to allow me to perform both a patented Cher head and neck flip, and to tuck my terrycloth hair behind my ear with my hand, when either move was needed for emphasis in a song performance.

With dance moves I had memorized by studying the television program *Zoom,* I executed riveting concerts for my horrified parents and enthusiastic sister. My performances were always a surprise. To begin, I would stick one leg into the doorway of the living room where my unsuspecting family was sitting. I shook the exposed leg until someone noticed, then in my best emcee voice, I announced Rosie Red was back in town for one last performance, and high kicked my way into the room. Using my mother's pink Avon hairbrush as a microphone, I sang songs from *42nd Street, The Wiz, and West Side Story*, as well as whatever songs were requested from my audience, which usually included something by Cher, Dolly Parton, and Dad's favorite, Charlie Pride.

Sadly, for whatever reasons, Rosie Red slowly faded over the years until she no longer performed in the Stewart home. She drifted to that place where other childhood activities retire, along with my bicycle, Star Wars action figures, countless colorful plastic pegs from a Lite-Brite, and a few stray Legos.

Much later, after leaving my small mountain hometown in southeastern Kentucky, I attended my first touring Broadway musical. *Dreamgirls* was electrifying, and it immediately rekindled my inner Rosie Red. Over the next few years, I made up for lost time. I attended shows anywhere and everywhere I could, including the Holy Lands of New York City and London. I saw many great theatre legends, each of them giving amazing performances, never disappointing the audience.

One of the greats who had eluded me, however, was Bernadette Peters. I was a lifelong fan of Bernadette. I owned her albums, watched her movies, and was guaranteed to watch any television show on which she made a guest appearance. But to my dismay, I had never seen her perform live on stage.

My luck changed when I received an email from a charity in Cincinnati, Ohio, announcing that Bernadette Peters would be performing a special concert for their spring fundraising gala. I read the email three times, then stared at the picture of Ms. Peters dressed in a full-length sequined gown, seductively sitting atop a grand piano. Her head was tilted back and her long, curly red hair cascaded down over her shoulders. She was holding a microphone and was looking out of my computer screen directly at me, as if to say, "Hurry, Keith. Buy the tickets so I can sing just for you."

That look was all it took for me to purchase not only tickets, but VIP passes granting my husband, Andy, and me access to a post-concert party and the opportunity to meet Bernadette herself. I clicked the purchase button, printed the tickets, and yelled for Andy to come hear the news. I was so excited I could barely get the words out of my mouth, and when I did, they were fast and unintelligible, "OhmygodIjustboughtticketstoseeBernadettePetersinconcert,"
I rambled.
"AndIgotVIPpassessowecanactuallymeetheraftertheconcert."
Ending with,
"hervoiceisjustwonderfulhaveItoldyoushestarsinoneofmyalltimefavoritemovies?!"

Andy smiled and told me it sounded great as he slowly backed his way out of the room. Breaking the stereotype of the modern gay man, Andy prefers working outdoors, playing poker with the fellas, and drinking beer. He does not share my love for all things Broadway, and is fearful of the look in my eyes and tone of my voice when I get as excited as I was at the prospect of meeting Bernadette Peters.

The weeks preceding the concert were filled with preparations. New outfits, including new underwear, socks, and shoes were a must. They had to be perfect: not too fancy, not too plain. Nothing that screamed, "I have purchased a new outfit," but nothing that looked like I had pulled it out of the back of my closet either. Respect to Ms. Peters had to be shown in every detail.

By far, the most important thing I needed to prepare was what I would say to Bernadette when I met her at the VIP reception. I knew we would only have a few minutes with her in the receiving line, so I would have to be witty, charming, clever, and sincere right out of the gate. I needed to hit her with the full Keith Stewart, and I needed to hit her hard. I just knew I would make such an impression she would have her assistant pull me out of the crowd later and invite me back to her hotel for an after-party. There we would sip champagne and she would sing show tunes to me. I implemented my understanding of the power of positive thinking to the hilt, and totally convinced myself the night of the concert would end with Bernadette and me hanging out in her suite, dressed as twins in hotel-issued cotton bathrobes, sharing popcorn, and giggling while watching an adult pay-per-view on the hotel television.

I wrote and rewrote my greeting to Bernadette many times during the days leading up to the event. Andy suggested it may be good for me to practice my lines with him. He could give me different potential responses that Ms. Peters might have so I would be ready for whatever she threw at me. But, I just couldn't. I had to save the actual words for the magical night. If I said them out loud to anyone other than the lady herself, the mojo might leak out entirely. I tried to explain this to Andy, who shook his head in a somewhat disapproving look and left me with my notebook full of scribbled potential icebreakers and went back to digging his new outdoor fire pit.

By the evening of the gala, my positive thinking had manifested into the delusion that I was on the verge of becoming best friends with Bernadette Peters. I was so worked up during our dinner right before the show I said to Andy I could not wait for Bernadette to meet me, and soon I would have my first celebrity friend. Andy tried one last attempt at convincing me to rehearse what I intended to say to her, but I refused. There was no need; fate was on my side.

The concert was everything I imagined it would be and more. Ms. Peters' voice was crisp and melodic, her charm was fetching, and her style was impeccable. I laughed. I cried. Mostly, I rehearsed what I would say to my new best friend at the VIP party. As soon as the show was over and the encore was finishing up, I started pushing Andy out of the auditorium. The fact that we were in the middle of a row did not matter. We "excuse me'd" our way out to the aisle, stepping on feet and purses, and hustled to the VIP reception room so we could be one of the first in line to meet Bernadette Peters.

It took half an hour or so for Bernie, which was now my pet name for her, to arrive at the reception. During our wait, I stayed in the receiving line, my feet firmly planted, my knees locked, and my arms at the ready if anyone tried to cut in front of us. I had the look of a person who was left alone in a dark haunted house waiting for a ghost to grab him. Andy tried to calm my nerves by bringing me a couple of cocktails from the bar. The gin felt warm as it slid down my throat, but instead of soothing me, it only invigorated me, and heightened my awareness of what was about to happen.

At last, Bernie arrived. She had changed into another stunning, tightly fitting sequined gown. She was petite and fragile as she glided into the room as only a Broadway diva can do, smiling and nodding to her adoring fans. The receiving line began moving as fans began doling out lame compliments to Bernie, and she began her gracious tolerance of these poor yahoos. There was no connection between her and any of them, nothing like the chemistry and witty repartee that we would soon share.

Suddenly we were next in line. My mind was racing. My palms were sweaty. The old lady in front of us who was blabbering to Bernie moved on, and it was our turn. I let Andy go first. He shook her hand, told her what a big fan he was and that he really enjoyed her performance tonight. She smiled and said thank you, an average response to a somewhat boring greeting, if you ask me. He took a step to the side and nodded for me to come forward. It was time for my moment, the beginning of a beautiful friendship with Bernadette Peters.

Always good under pressure, I rose to the occasion and took Bernie's hand in mine, smiled and said, "You probably will never guess what my favorite movie role of yours was."

Bernie was charmed; she cocked her head back and flirtingly arched an eyebrow saying, "What?" (*Oh my God. This was working. She was my new BFF.*)

"Your role in *Blazing Saddles*," I said.

Crickets. I heard nothing but crickets. It was as if everyone at the VIP party stopped what they were doing, gasped, and then stared at me. Something had gone terribly wrong, but I was unsure what. Was the movie a flop? I was pretty sure it was one of Mel Brooks' more successful movies. Did she have a scandalous affair with Mr. Brooks on the set that I didn't know about? Had I already committed a faux pas with my new BFF? Bernie blankly looked at me, the smile long gone from her face, and said "I wasn't in *Blazing Saddles*."

Now, on hearing that, some people may have said something like, "Oh, oops, I'm terribly sorry," and left, but not me. I was so confused. I could have sworn it was her. All my life I thought it was her. I convinced myself in that split second that Bernie was mistaken. Why she has been in so many things she has just forgotten! So I said, "Yes, yes, remember, you were in it."

"No. I wasn't. I was in *The Jerk*," she curtly responded. Quite frankly, if truth be known, the way she inflected her words when she said *The Jerk* rubbed me the wrong way. I could not believe I was already having a spat with my new BFF Bernie. This spontaneous public rebuff by Ms. Peters stoked the long-dormant embers of my own inner diva, Rosie Red, and when fully fired up, Rosie could hold her own with any two-bit stage performer.

So I tried again, "You were in it. I even know the song you sang in it." As Rosie Red took full control of me, I had what I think is medically termed an out of body experience, and broke into song for Bernadette, singing the tune "I'm Tired" to everyone around me while gesturing a signal with my arms that encouraged others to join in.

No one did. They chose, instead, to watch with opened mouths the debacle happening in front of them. Bernadette finally said, "That was Madeline Kahn, and she was great in that, but it *wasn't me*." She then made some slight gesture with her hand and two large men dressed in black came from nowhere and told Andy and me it was time to move on. Before they could remove us, however, I insisted they wait until we took our picture with Bernie, although at that moment I was beginning to feel the first tingling's of humiliation prick my psyche. The picture was snapped with Bernie barely grinning, my face blood red, and Andy looking horrified. As Andy grabbed my arm and pulled me away, I looked over my shoulder once more at my ex-BFF and said, "Say what you want, but I know you were in it." But I knew at that moment she had not been in it. It had been Madeline Kahn all along, yet for some reason I couldn't give in to her. Perhaps it was the combination of gin, humiliation, and regret. Or the knowledge that I would not end my evening giving manis and pedis to my new best friend Bernadette Peters. Possibly, it was the long, detailed explanation Andy would expect from my outburst. All I knew for sure was that I, and especially Rosie Red who was never wrong, could not let it go, and could not give in to smug little Bernie and her security team.

Thankfully, the VIP ticket also included an open bar where we headed to let my breakdown commence. I searched in vain for a cloth napkin or perhaps a stray bar towel large enough to throw on my head and allow Rosie enough hair to give one of her trademarked ear-tucks or even a full-on head and neck flip. Over another cocktail, I ignored the flood of onlookers staring at me as if I were a circus side-show, and racked my brain trying to figure out where I had gone wrong in my positive thinking exercises. Andy suggested it wasn't my positive thinking, but rather lack of knowledge that had led us to this point. I responded that gin made him rude. What I knew for sure was that Bernadette Peters and I were not destined to be friends or even acquaintances. She hated me, and I wasn't that crazy about her anymore. We had grown apart.

As we left the theatre, I saw a large poster advertising next year's gala event. The scheduled performer was none other than Ms.

Patti LuPone. Patti LuPone is a diva among divas. She is the very epitome of the Broadway stage. I poked Andy in the arm, jotting down the date and telephone number for tickets on a napkin and said, "Patti LuPone. Now there's a gal who knows how to be a friend." And Rosie Red silently agreed.

Free Range Bird

I am obsessed with food, and not in the way that immediately comes to mind when a fat man types those words. I am constantly reading labels and trying to find organic products on my quest to be a healthy person. My normal diet is mostly vegetarian, and I have even considered going vegan (ok, I have read about the vegan lifestyle). I am a member of a CSA—community supported agriculture—farm, which basically means I get large baskets of fresh, locally grown, organic fruit and vegetables each week without having to actually tend a farm.

Regardless of how much I support local farms, I still have to go the grocery store each week for a lot of my food, and even then, I still try to buy organic products. Living in the Appalachian Mountains in a rural Kentucky town seriously hinders this effort. You don't find much locally grown baby bok choy in the produce aisle at the Sav-A-Lot or the Piggly Wiggly.

As a result, not only do I have to leave the local farms and mom-and-pop grocery stores behind, but I also have to shop at the giant mega-grocery stores. Don't get me wrong, I love a good outing to Sam's Club or Costco and buying huge bulk items, usually large pallets of dog food to feed our normal sized Dudley and the horse-who-thinks-he-is-a-dog, Duke. Plus, there is a certain comfort in knowing that I will have enough olive oil to supply my entire cul-de-sac or that I will not run out of toilet paper should my entire household get stricken with a nasty stomach virus.

My main concern about these high-ceilinged superstores can be boiled down into two words: trapped birds. I am deathly afraid of these trapped birds. You all have noticed them. They are always there, lurking. You are minding your own business, trying to decide on which flavor of Hamburger Helper to buy when suddenly it does a fly by. You know the stupid bird is scared to death. He probably just flew into the Walmart supercenter to grab one of those bird-seed concoctions molded into the shape of a bell for dinner when he lost his bearings. He can't find his way out of the store, and he is now in panic mode. The saying "bird brain" was invented for a reason: they have small ones, and they don't use what they have that well.

Why be scared of such a tiny bird? Why be so bitter towards a poor, struggling animal? Perhaps I am overreacting, you say? I beg to differ. A couple of years ago, I was accosted by an angry, terrified bird in a Kroger MegaGrand Store. I honestly can say I will never be the same, and neither will that dumb bird. Here's how it went down:

I ran into the grocery after work to pick up a few items. For convenience, I stopped at the store that was closer to work, so it was not my home Kroger. All the produce was placed in completely different places, and I walked around aimlessly trying to find the organic section, in particular, the celery. I was standing in front of a large display of carefully pyramided cantaloupe when out of the corner of my eye, I spotted something dark and ominous. It was a bird, maybe a sparrow, flying at what appeared to be the speed of a fully engrossed Indy car. I stood there and thought to myself, "Huh, that bird looks like it's flying directly toward me." The next thing I know I feel something repeatedly beating me about the head and ear, and I hear the FLAP FLAP FLAP of bird wings. "OH GOD! HELP ME!" I yelled, flailing both arms up in the air trying to fight off the crazed bird. I was feeling around for a celery stalk to use as a sword, and in my panic, I jumped back directly into the large display of cantaloupe. At this point, the bird had tired of terrorizing me and had flown away to target its next victim over in the dairy section, but I was still flailing my arms, rolling in the floor with about fifty cantaloupes.

After I was sure I was bird-free, I looked around at the scene. Gasping and out of breath, I was on my knees surrounded by a sea of cantaloupe, some still whole but most cracked open and oozing. My hair was tousled, my shirt had come untucked, and I was clutching my organic celery sword as if my life depended on it. The lady who had been restocking the iceberg lettuce rushed over to me while all the other shoppers in the produce section stared as if I'd just decided to do a back flip into the cantaloupe for no reason at all, like I was some sort of freakish, produce trouble maker. "Sir, are you ok?!" the lady asked. I couldn't respond. I was incredibly embarrassed and just wanted to get out of the store.

I tried to maintain some level of grace, and finally told the woman, "Someone ought to do something about that bird." She looked around either trying to see the bird or to look for security. Regardless, I could tell she did not believe I had been attacked. "Did you not see it?" I asked incredulously.

"Um, yes sir, yes," she said as she helped me to my feet.

I made my way to the check-out getting madder with each step. That stupid bird had totally punked me right there in the produce section. He had done it so quickly and stealth-like that no one else had apparently even seen it. Stupid bird. Everyone just thought I was a big goober who had attacked the fresh fruit. Argh, that bird! I knew he was somewhere in the rafters of the store looking at me and laughing. I decided to gather what was left of my dignity and pay for my celery (no cantaloupe) and go home. Thank goodness this was not my home Kroger store.

The entire time my items were being scanned and bagged, the clerk kept looking at my shirt. I thought she had a look on her face that said, "I really want to laugh right now, but I will wait until you leave." I assumed she had seen the incident, so I just ignored her. When I looked down to swipe my debit card, I noticed it. That bird—that vile, evil bird—had pooped all over my maroon button down. The stark white mess went from my shoulder, down my arm, and glared like it would glow-in-the dark against the color of my shirt. I looked up immediately and scanned the ceiling. I think I said something like, "You people need to get your bird problem under control," to the clerk and then marched out the door, horrified.

So heed my warning, when you see a bird trapped inside a large store, be very careful. Know that it is stupid. Know that it is vicious. Know that it is ticked off because it's too dumb to find the exit, and it's looking to make someone pay. You do not want to end up being on the security camera blooper reel at the Kroger Employee Christmas Party. I have been there, and it ain't pretty.

Monkey in the Mirror

I like to please other people. I always have, and always will. I don't mind lending a helping hand to anyone who needs it. There are those folks, however, who truly don't care if they please others. They do and say exactly as they want, regardless of the consequences and resulting fallout. I always look at these people with a bit of awe and a lot of pity. I just can't understand not wanting to make others happy. Don't get me wrong, I will stand up for myself and what I believe in, but in social situations, I would never purposely offend someone. So, when people ask if I like the new paint color they have painted their living room, I always enthusiastically say, "Yes," even if the walls look like a baby used the wall for its own personal bathroom. If asked at a party if I would help get the hors d'oeuvres from the oven, I say, "Sure thing," even if I really would prefer to just sit with the other guests and chat.

Basically, what I am saying is I'm just a nice guy.

If I had to choose only one person to make happy, though, it would be my mom. I've always been a mama's boy, and continue to be one in my mid-forties. Mother has always been the one to take my side, even when she knew there was no way I was winning a particular fight. We have always been two peas in a pod.

As a little boy, I loved to watch my mother get ready for work in the mornings. I would sit in the bathroom with her while she applied her makeup, tried to tame her curly hair, and generally prepared herself for a new day. I was fascinated by all the tools she used in order to make herself look like "Mom." The weirdest was some kind of silver tong-looking apparatus with a scissor-like handle with two holes for your fingers. She used it to squeeze her eyelashes and raise her eyelids. I was never sure exactly what that did for her, but I knew it grossed me out.

I also kept a close eye on her pink Avon hairbrush, as it had a secret double life. Whenever I performed my private, hush-hush "shows" in front of my bedroom mirror while listening to Cher and K-Tel albums, I would sneak in the brush. It made the perfect sized microphone for my tiny hand. No wonder Avon dominated the beauty world in the 70's.

Mom also used a blue plastic hand mirror daily. Many times, she would see me sitting on the bathroom toilet watching her work on herself, and would smile and hold the mirror down in front of my face for me to see. As I looked at my reflection in it, mom would say, "See the monkey in the mirror?" and laugh. Being a person who innately wants to make others happy, I would always say, "Ha! Ha! Ha! Yeah! I see it!" However, the truth was I did not see a monkey. I saw a very cute little boy with black curly hair and hazel eyes, and a 1970's autumn gold colored bathroom in the background.

Each time she said it, I furiously scanned the mirror for a monkey. I looked along the blue plastic lining the glass, thinking it was hidden, like an early version of a "Where's Waldo" puzzle. I tried with all my might to see it, because she so obviously saw a monkey there. Of all people, I did not want to make her feel bad and tell her I didn't see it, and that I suspected the monkey was only in her mind.

This cycle went on for years, and each time I would search and search for the monkey, never finding it. Sometimes, after my mother left for work and my grandmother, who babysat me, settled in to watch her "stories" on television, I would go back to the bathroom, grab the mirror, and really examine it in hopes of finding the monkey. I suppose part of my obsession with the monkey was not just pleasing my mother, but also proving to myself she was not totally insane.

Here was this poor woman, trying to be a good mother and wife to her family while helping run a family business, and she was so delusional she saw monkeys in places they did not exist. I wondered if she saw monkeys at work or in her car. Maybe it had something to do with all those devices she used to get ready, like the tong-like device that pulled open her eyelids? Of course, being a nice guy, I would never be so rude as to mention my concerns to my crazy mother. Instead, I would continue playing along and telling her I, too, saw the monkeys. As long the craziness was kept at a low-level of only seeing small primates, what could it hurt? I never mentioned to my mother I could not and never had seen a monkey in that blue mirror. I kept the secret of the monkey for years. I would not betray my Mom's possible mental illness.

Then, one summer when I was in my early 20's, I was home from college. I rummaged around in the bathroom looking for something in the depths of the shelves underneath the sink. As I moved a few items around, I saw it. The blue hand mirror. I couldn't believe it had been relegated to the junk shelves. I suppose with the 1980's came the lighted three-way mirror making mom's blue monkey hand mirror no longer needed in her morning ritual. I pulled out the blue plastic and held it in my hands. It was like finding a rare buried treasure. I said to myself, "You are 21 years old. You can find that monkey in this mirror now," and with a determination I had never known, I sat down in the floor of the bathroom and starting searching.

After five or so minutes, a light bulb went off above my head. Surely, it couldn't be what I was thinking. There's just no way. She was referring to my reflection?! She thought she was being funny?! I was the monkey in the mirror?! Is this what she had meant all the time?!

In what can only be called a rage, I stomped into the family room with the mirror. My mother sat reading a book. "I AM THE MONKEY?! I AM THE MONKEY?!" I yelled. She blankly looked at me. I then waved the blue mirror in her face and screamed, "I AM THE MONKEY IN THE MIRROR? SEE THE MONKEY IN THE MIRROR, KEITH? I AM THE MONKEY? IS THIS WHAT YOU MEANT ALL THIS TIME?"

Mother just sat there, obviously not sure what to say or do. Her gestures were slow and calculated as if she were talking down an angry bear. Finally, she said, "Keith Allen, are you serious? Of course you were the monkey in the mirror. That is crazy. Who the Hell else would it have been?" I explained to her all the time and anguish I'd spent over the years trying to find the monkey so I could prove her saneness. She just looked stiffly at me until she finally had taken all she could, bursting into a laughter that filled the house. The laughter just added insult to my injury. I stormed out of the room and headed to my bedroom, mumbling about monkeys.

I spent the rest of my evening sulking by myself; mom spent hers on the phone calling everyone in our family and telling them what a boob I was as she wiped tears from her eyes.

If I had ever envied those people who didn't have a predisposition to please others, it was that very moment. If I had been that type of guy, I would have told Mother in 1975 there was no monkey in the mirror and she needed to get some help. Then, the pink Avon hairbrush and I would have retired to my bedroom to sing my favorite songs, "I Love the Nightlife" and "Half Breed." But, noooo, I wanted to please her. I HAD to please others. I couldn't help it then, and I can't help it now, but one's thing's for sure—I no longer blindly answer ridiculous questions asked by my sadistic mother.

Luck, Be a Lady Tonight

I walked into the casino like I owned the place. I was still basking in the afterglow of having just seen my all-time favorite singer, Wynonna Judd, in concert minutes earlier at the French Lick Resort and Casino in French Lick, Indiana. I was looking good, I was feeling confident, and I was ready to employ *The Secret* in order to win back the cash I had spent on this weekend jaunt to the north side of the Mason-Dixon Line—a place I rarely ever speak of, let alone go.

The Secret's secret is positive thinking. You must send out good and positive thoughts of whatever it is you desire in order to receive said desire from the Universe. If you want a new car, you visualize yourself driving that new car. If you want to win back the cash you laid out to see Wynonna in concert in the nether regions of Indiana, you visualize two hundred dollars in quarters falling out of a slot machine while a lights flash above your head and a siren blares. In my particular visualization, I also pictured confetti falling from the ceiling and a sash that read "Casino Slot Winner" being pinned to my shirt.

Our first stop in the casino was the customer service desk to sign up for our rewards card. I am sure these cards are handy and helpful to a regular gambler, but not so much for me. For one, I very likely will never be back in French Lick, Indiana, and for two, I don't think gambling away two hundred dollars will garner enough bonus points to amount to anything; but Andy had discovered you received a free t-shirt if you signed up, so the decision was made then and there to get the card. There is very little we won't do for a free t-shirt. Andy was in front of me and his application was quickly processed, his t-shirt was dispensed, and he was free to gamble the night away. During my turn, there was a computer glitch, and the entire system had to be re-booted, taking at least five minutes. After the computers were restarted and running, the clerk discovered he needed to change the receipt paper in the machine before he could activate my card. This delay was too much for Andy. With dollar signs in place of pupils in his eyes, he mumbled something about not waiting for me anymore and going to play poker. When I turned around to ask what he had said, he was gone. When I finally received my card and t-shirt, I was mortified to find the shirt was bright orange—the shade hunters wear so they will not shoot each other in the forest. It was then dropped into a plastic sack and handed to me, and I was sent on my way.

I always think of casinos as sexy places. People are dressed up, there is excitement and desperation in the air, free liquor is flowing, and there is a sexual charge lingering. Mind you, this is based on Las Vegas casinos. I had never been to the casino in French Lick, Indiana, when I formed this theory.

As I wandered around getting my bearings, I noticed that while some of the other patrons looked nice, the majority of them had not dressed up. In fact, I began to wonder if part of the hotel had a fire alarm drill and made the guests immediately leave their rooms, with no time to change from their pajamas. It appeared they were waiting in the casino until they received the "all clear" and could return to bed. There was also no free liquor flowing. You were expected to pay for all drinks no matter how much money you were throwing away at the tables. As Julia Roberts says to the snotty sales clerk in Pretty Woman, "Big Mistake. Big. Huge." If I am completely sober, there is no way in hell I am going to overspend at a casino. Do these people know nothing?! As far as feeling sexy myself, no matter how good the outfit you are wearing, a grey plastic sack holding a bright orange t-shirt kills all sexiness.

The casino had a special room designated for "Non-Smokers." I was very excited to see this and immediately headed there. When I walked into the room, it was clear it was for the uncool gamblers. The losers in the non-smoking room looked like they were there for a Sci-Fi convention or a Pocket Protectors of America meeting. Part of being a gambler is the willingness to take chances. You must lose big if you want to win big. Smokers take chances with their health every time light up a cigarette. They have always been rebels, and sometimes, in certain situations, smoking is just cool. If you aren't willing to smoke in a casino, then you must be willing to inhale a little secondhand smoke if you want to run with the big dogs. To prove my point, a cluster of slot machines in the smoking section of the casino was giving away a brand new Camaro as a grand prize. The same cluster of machines in the non-smoking section? Giving away a Kia. I'm not sure, but it looked used. Seeing this, I turned and rushed from the room before any of the cool gamblers saw me.

I settled in at a row of slot machines that cost one dollar to play. That is big money to me, and is as high as I am willing to go when betting. My father thinks he is a gambling expert. He is one of the luckiest people alive, and he only plays a certain kind of slot machine. He has passed this knowledge down to me, and I try to find this type of machine whenever I play. His advice also includes staking out a machine that someone is currently playing, keeping an eye on it until the person leaves, and then immediately grabbing it. His theory is if the sap before you fed the machine a lot of money and it didn't pay out for him, then it is due to pay. It sounds pretty solid as far as gambling tips go, so I always go with it.

Still using *The Secret* philosophy, I sat down in a chair left empty when a downtrodden lady had scooted away after spending all her money and not winning anything. As I fed the machine my money, I visualized myself sitting in the Camaro and having the winner's sash pinned to my shirt while people cheered for me. I was trying to focus and be positive, but all I could hear was the horrible music from the sound system blaring in my ears. For some reason, the casino was playing Sir-Mix-A-Lot's, "Jump On It," at a remarkably high volume. For those of you who aren't familiar with Sir-Mix-A-Lot, he is the artist who brought us the unforgettable, "I like big butts and I cannot lie," song. In this ditty, he repeats the words, "JUMP ON IT," a gazillion times. The most troubling part, though, was the older man—I am going to say around the age of seventy—who was singing along with every word. After losing twenty dollars in less than five minutes, I decided to find another machine with less distractions and better mojo.

Little did I know, however, no better mojo would be found on this particular night. Lady Luck would be an elusive battle ax to me, laughing at my misfortune and taking my money. As my cash dwindled, I moved from the slot machines that promised a new Camaro down to the cluster offering a nine-thousand-dollar payout, and eventually to the few cheap ones whose grand prize was an off-road four-wheeler. If you know me at all, you know the last thing I would ever need is a four-wheeler, but I told myself I now own a hunter's orange t-shirt. Why not wear it in to the woods on a four-wheeler? It didn't matter. Those machines took my money as fast as the fancy ones.

I knew I had hit bottom when I looked around at my fellow gamblers playing the same slot machines in my row. My evening had started in the dollar slots with people who were relatively nice looking and presentable, but now I was sandwiched between a terribly flatulent man who looked remarkably like the Unabomber and a younger guy wearing a t-shirt that read "Five Dollar Footlong," with an arrow pointing to his undercarriage. The final straw came when a couple sat down across from me, and the lady proceeded to explain the slot machine game to the man. Not the different pay outs, but the game itself. How do you not know how a slot machine works? He was even asking her questions.

"So if there are two sevens on the line but the other seven is down below, what does that mean?"

"Oh honey, it means you don't win."

"But I have two out of three."

"You have to have all three."

"Are you sure? That doesn't sound right to me."

"Well, honey, we could ask."

I knew then and there if I stayed I would be the person they asked for help, and my nerves were not up for it. I hopped up, found Andy (whose night had gone as poorly as mine), and we began our walk of shame out of the casino.

As we made our way to the exit, Andy looked sweetly over at me. I thought he was going to say just the right thing to make me feel better. Something like, "I'm a winner, I have you," or "I don't need to gamble, you are my grand prize." But, instead, he smiled and said the following words:

"Your pants are unzipped."

A Horse Is a Horse, Of Course of Course

Horse and carriage rides are a staple in urban tourism. Nearly every city has at least a few in its historic district. You can find them in every shape and size. I have been in a cozy buggy for two in New York City, and a mass transit carriage carrying twenty in New Orleans. They can be the perfect romantic setting for a date or simply a way to rest your feet and sightsee in a chosen town.

A few years ago, my parents were attending a conference in Cincinnati, Ohio. They had chosen to stay just across the Ohio River in Covington, KY, in order to have a view of the Cincinnati skyline during their visit. Their hotel was directly on the river, offered beautiful views of the city, and tried its best to make its guests forget they were staying in Covington, KY. Covington, even with the spectacular river view, has always had a reputation as a city in which you did not want to be caught by yourself late at night. Whether this was still true was beside the point, because Mama Stewart was told this all her life and believed it. Once her mind was made up, no urban revitalization or gentrification would change it.

I lived in Lexington at the time, about an hour and a half from Covington. My parents invited me up for dinner their final night in town, so I drove up to spend some family time with them.

After we had eaten dinner, I noticed there was a horse-drawn carriage sitting in front of the hotel. I thought it would be such a good idea for us to take a little tour of the area. Maybe this would convince my mother that Covington had cleaned up its act and was not such a bad place after all. I mean, if they are taking innocent tourists around the city streets on a horse, how bad can it be?

Naturally, Mom was reluctant to go. My dad was all for it, so I kept insisting until my mom gave in and agreed. We all three piled in, and a nice young lady named Cindy said she would be our host/driver. She then introduced us to Bill the Horse. Bill the Horse looked a little worse for wear. His eyes seemed to dart about and he kept jerking and stomping his feet. He looked as nervous as if he were getting ready to run a race, not stroll the historic streets of Covington.

Of course, my knowledge of horses was minimal, so I couldn't be sure what an average horse working in this job looked like. Even though I was born and bred in Kentucky, I was from Appalachia, not the Bluegrass area of the state. The closest I had been to a horse was a donkey basketball in elementary school—a fundraiser of some sort where two teams played a basketball game while riding donkeys (don't ask, I can't explain it either).

So, even as I thought to myself that Bill the Horse looked shifty, I didn't feel confident enough to mention it to my parents. We hopped into the carriage, left the well-lit street in front of the hotel, and rounded the corner into the dark depths of Covington. Cindy was very knowledgeable about the historic city, entertaining us with whimsical stories of the Germans who had settled here along the Ohio River, and who had built the charming German-like bell clock tower in the town square.

I was relaxed, and quite confident that Mama Stewart was finally seeing the charm and character of this Kentucky river town. Suddenly, without warning, Bill the Horse made a shrieking noise and jerked his head. Whatever caused this pain was relentless as he then raised both front legs off the ground, snorted, and took off as if he'd been called to the post at the Kentucky Derby. Cindy, who was in the middle of telling us about the town square cuckoo clock, cut her story short and yelled, "Oh my God!! Biilllll!!"

Thus began a three-minute ride of terror through the streets of Covington in a carriage being pulled by a psychotic horse. The only thing my parents and I could do was hunker down, hold on, and pray for daylight. Cindy was screaming enough for all of us. Finally, the back wheel of the wagon became so loose and wobbly that it slowed the carriage to the point that even Bill the Horse couldn't continue his rampage through town. Cindy eventually convinced him to stop on the side of the street. We had been dragged probably a mile or so off the scheduled tour path, and from the looks of things around us, we were exactly in the spot of Covington my mother had always warned me about and knew existed.

Cindy had calmed down Bill the Horse and discovered his bit, a device that goes inside the horse's mouth, had slipped and was causing him pain. Apparently, horrific pain. She smoothed his mane and gently talked to him, then turned to us and asked if we would exit the carriage so she could work on the wheel.

Cindy tightened the bolts and screws and declared the carriage safe again. "Folks, Bill the Horse and I apologize for the delay, but we are now ready to continue our tour," she said with a forced smile. Just as we started for the carriage, Bill the Horse had another pain. With the same jerk and yelp, he started running again. Evidently, the bit had slipped into the wrong area of his mouth again. Cindy was standing behind the wagon, and just like in the movies, she ran to the side and hopped up onto her seat in the carriage. I was very impressed with her until I realized she had no idea how to stop Bill the Horse. The last we saw of Cindy was her riding the out-of-control carriage being pulled by a galloping Bill the Horse. "Soooorrrrryyyyyyy!" she yelled as they rounded a corner.

We were left on the streets of Covington alone, disoriented, and stunned. After a few minutes, we determined taxis did not frequent this part of town, nor did many cars at all for that matter. Finally, my dad made the decision we should just start walking towards the river and eventually we would find the hotel. No one laughed when I suggested we stop at one of the many package stores we passed and buy ourselves a forty-ouncer for the trip, although Mom's nerves were so frazzled I think she may have wanted one.

An hour later, sweaty, scared, and still stunned, we found the hotel. Because it was my idea to take the ride in the first place, it was deemed my fault that Bill the Horse went crazy. Both my parents concluded family time was over, and suggested I just go on back to Lexington and leave them be.

I never saw Bill the Horse again, but I still think of him. Every time I see a white horse gently pulling loads of people around a downtown area while they gaze at antebellum homes or newly developed parks, I check for a bit on the horse. Those tours may look care free, but one wrong step and your pleasant ride could turn into your own personal Derby.

The Graveyard Mafia

Family. The dictionary will tell you the word means any group of persons closely related by blood as parents, children, uncles, aunts, and cousins. When you read the definition, it seems like such a harmless and calm word. It makes it hard to believe that a family could be completely co-dependent on each other, down to the last cousin. Or that the family unit itself can take on a life of its own, clouding the thoughts and actions of each individual within the group. Or that the dynamics of the group can put the "fun" in the word "dysfunctional." Yet, those extra definitions are exactly how my family should be defined.

Perhaps it is my Appalachian roots that help grow the strong bonds of my family. Appalachians have a robust tradition of closely knit families who depend on each other for not only their social life, but also their very existence. While my extended family is very much modern and sophisticated, we all maintain our southeastern Kentucky mountain ways. We may live in cities, but scratch us, and the hillbilly will bleed.

My cousins and I all have strong personalities, and are all very competitive. Each of us has the potential for unruly behavior on our own, but this potential is magnified when any two of us are together. Knowing that, it probably makes perfect sense to read that when a group of us congregate anything can happen. Nothing can be ruled out. When we have family get-togethers, it is usually an evening of seeing who can get their point across by talking the loudest. To people outside the family, this can look like a massive argument, but only rarely does that happen. Because of our tendency for rambunctiousness, I nicknamed my partners in family crime the Crazy Cousins.

Although we have tried to reign ourselves in and behave—especially in public or in front of outsiders—we have never quite mastered that skill. Quite frankly, we often come across as just simply, "too much."

For instance, the first time I introduced my partner to the Crazy Cousins, they immediately took his pack of cigarettes away from him to keep for themselves. Then, as if that wasn't enough, they told him if he did anything to Keith that they didn't like, they would, "gut him like a fish." Like I said, sometimes we're too much.

Don't get me wrong, most of the time, we are a harmless bunch. Live and let live. We know that, if measured, we would read a little heavy on the, "crazy scale," and we gladly admit it. We also love to talk about one another, and there is usually a family squabble going on at all times, perpetuated by the prodding of a Crazy Cousin not directly involved in the fight. But one thing is for certain, when an outside force messes with any of us, the ranks are closed in, the wagons are circled, and this bunch morphs into one insane fighting machine. This fact, coupled with a tendency to be, "too much," can often lead to dark days.

Our most dysfunctional crazy moment came at a family funeral a few years ago for one of the family spouses (read in-law). During the service at the chapel, there was a moment when people could come up and say a few words about the dearly departed. A couple of the Crazy Cousins stepped forward and said a few words intending to be witty. They jokingly said, "When Freddy married Lori, he told us he just wasn't going to like us, that he barely liked his own sisters and had no desire to like anyone else's." Most everyone took the words in the spirit they were intended, laughed, and moved on. However, the sisters of the departed didn't think the comment was funny at all, and secretly stewed in anger the remainder of the ceremony (I mean, honestly?!).

The funeral then proceeded to the graveside service. The prayers were given, the flowers placed on the casket, and the service ended. People were milling about, speaking and greeting each other, reminding everyone which house would be hosting the after-funeral food.

Suddenly, from out of nowhere, loud, harsh words are heard being shouted. The entire crowd looked around to see one member of the dearly departed's family (again, read in-laws) with her finger in one of the Crazy Cousin's faces (that, by the way, is something that one should never, ever do). The words became more and more heated until we eventually saw a shove. The woman with the finger actually shoved a Crazy Cousin! At the grave site! At a funeral!

Seeing a Crazy Cousin being shoved triggered a reaction similar to the old Wonder Twins cartoons when the Twins transform themselves into super heroes. One Crazy Cousin standing to the west of the incident seemingly said, "Crazy Cousin powers activate, into the form of a cheetah," and then covered the twenty or so feet in a split second to get to the melee. Another Crazy Cousin already in her car to the north activated, "into the form of fire," and spread herself at an alarmingly fast rate to the war zone. From all directions of the compass the Crazy Cousins converged. However, so did the even crazier family of the departed. In fact, they were *so* crazy, it needs to be spelled Krazy!

I stood with my sister staring at all this for a moment. She had a baby in her arms and was unable to activate her powers, so she looked at me in disbelief and yelled, "Are you not going?!" I quickly activated my Crazy Cousin power into the form of a steamroller and moved in.

When I got to the battlefield, I couldn't believe my eyes. People were actually brawling all around me at the graveside service. One Crazy Cousin had picked up a display of roses and was beating someone else around the head with the flowers…from the funeral…roses…used as a weapon.

It seemed all this was in slow motion. I was trying to maintain my wits, help stop the fight, and bring some order to the chaos.

Then it happened.

Someone knocked off my sunglasses.

"Oh, Hell No!" was my reaction, and funeral or not, all bets were off. I started blindly swinging at anyone not in my family. I won't say it was my proudest moment, but those were new sunglasses.

The fight went on for a few more minutes, and was finally broken up when the employees of the funeral home called the police. If they'd had a water hose, they would have turned it on us. Everyone at that point started to scatter to their cars. I will have to say that the other side, the Krazy family, got the worst end of the deal. The roses were a good weapon, and after many knocks around the head and ears, the Krazies were showing signs of defeat.

The Crazy Cousins and I drove to my aunt's home in silence. There was a little left over crying and aggression in the cars, but no one really said much of anything. Andy had gone directly to my aunt's after the chapel ceremony to prepare the food and get the buffet line in order, and in so doing, had missed the brawl.

As we all started walking in, dirty, tattered, hair askew, sleeves ripped, makeup smudged, he knew something was amiss. When I explained what had happened, he just stared at me. After seven years, he still had that look of horror and amusement that all outsiders get when witnessing my family for the first time. My Crazy Cousin's husband took in the entire thing and then said, "I sure didn't want to drive all the way from Ohio down here to this funeral today, but Crazy Cousin Wife made me, and I will tell you one thing, I'll never miss another family funeral."

Now, don't get me wrong. I do not condone fighting at a funeral. I do know that you might be a redneck if you fight at a funeral. But we didn't start the fight. We just finished it.

Don't judge me.

Baptism in Massage Oil

Thankfully, I do not have to admit I am wrong very often. Quite frankly, it just doesn't happen that much; and when it does, I am never the first to publicly acknowledge I am mistaken about a fact, incident, or issue. However, when backed into a corner, I will reluctantly admit the error of my ways and own the mistake. For instance, I fully admit I mistakenly pronounced the word "artisans", as in the Kentucky Artisans Center, as "Arteesian," for years. I also thought the lyrics to Def Leppard's 80's hit "Pour Some Sugar on Me" were, "sweet potatoes, sack of beans," when clearly to everyone else it says, "sweet to taste, sample me." So it is with great humbleness I say I was completely wrong in my opinion of massages and spa treatments.

I have never liked other people to touch me. The thought of it grosses me out. I remember in high school dreading walking down the hallway between classes because people would rub up against me. Crowded buses, subways, and trains always cause me great concern because of the closeness of my fellow passengers. Heaven forbid it's a hot day and other people's sweat becomes an issue.

I have had many offers for massages over the years, and I have always politely declined. Usually, these offers came from some poor soul who had decided to date me and my idiosyncrasies, thinking a great rubdown would somehow win me over. After explaining I didn't like to be touched at all, let alone massaged, it was usually just a matter of time before my suitor found a way to escape my web of oddities.

So it is indeed ironic that I would end up married to Andy, a man who is an old school massage lover. He likes Swedish, aromatherapy, deep tissue, and hot rock. He even likes that little Mr.

Happy thing they sell at Macy's during the Christmas season. He loves it all, and although he has never offered to give me one, he has always encouraged me to have a professional massage, just once. My best friend, Donna, would live at a spa if possible. She, too, has tried everything in her power to convince me this fear of mine was irrational and uncalled for. However, I remained unmoved and unshaken from my position of having no love for massages.

I'm not sure what circumstances caused me to agree to a long weekend at a rustic spa deep in the hills of eastern North Carolina, but for whatever reason, I found Andy and myself checking into a very quaint resort one spring Sunday evening in late May. One of the requirements of staying at this particular inn is that each patron agrees to two spa treatments during their stay. Andy was giddy, I was reluctant. While Andy dealt with the perky desk clerk, I poured over the spa menu trying to find the least invasive treatments for my two picks. I finally settled on the Men's Rescue Facial and a Hot Stone Relaxation Massage. Not wanting to do this spa thing half-assed, I went ahead and signed up for a third item, the Green Tea Body Detoxifying Wrap. What the hell, when in Rome, blah, blah, blah. And let's be honest, this body was in bad need of some detox.

After checking in, Meg, the perky clerk, gave us a brief orientation of the facility. She said THE television on the property was in the room behind us, and that was also THE room that had Wi-Fi. I suddenly felt the air being sucked out of the room. "I'm sorry, Meg, did you say that was the only television?" I asked.

It was.

"And internet is not available in our room? Just over there in the small TV room?"

"That's correct, sir," perky Meg explained. "We want you to be able to completely unplug and relax while you are here with us!"

Oh boy, this could get dicey. Sunday was *Game of Thrones* night on HBO, and I needed to be in constant contact with the worldwide web in case there was breaking entertainment news or I needed instant gratification to reinforce my weak self-esteem.

We left the office and drove up the hill to our room. I was pleasantly surprised to discover we had our own cottage with a full kitchen, eating area, living room, bedroom, bathroom, and front porch. The bed had excellent linens, and a big, puffy comforter. All the bath products in the room were Aveda. Very foo-foo, very shi-shi. Perhaps this wasn't going to be so bad after all.

I decided since I had signed up to have my body detoxed the following day, I was free to eat and drink whatever I chose for the evening. The resort offered a free wine and cheese reception for guests, and Andy and I hit it and hit it hard. We had several plates of cheese, meats, olives and nuts, washed down with some excellent homemade white wine sangria.

We later drove out to a local convenience store down the road for some ice and drinks to keep in our cottage. I discovered the country store offered a Southern junk food staple—rope pickled bologna. I threw caution to wind and asked for a few inches and some saltines. If I was paying for a detox, I wanted my money's worth.

The morning of the spa treatments, I began to get very nervous. What in the world was I thinking? I knew I did not like this sort of thing. Why had I let myself get talked into this? By the time I had worked myself into a frenzy big enough to leave, Trish, my therapist, came to get me for my facial.

I reluctantly walked into the treatment room with her. She spoke in a polite whisper and smelled like springtime. She instructed me to take off all my clothes and put them into a basket, lie down on the table, cover myself with the provided linen sheets, and get ready to relax. Her voice was hypnotic, and I fell into a trance. I just smiled and said, "OK." The next thing I knew I was lying naked on her table, covered with some sheets, listening to some very relaxing music while Trish was doing something magical with her fingers on my head and neck.

My original nervousness, however, began to creep back into play, and because I ramble when nervous, I began chatting with Trish. I talked about how hot the temperature was outside, how I wasn't a morning person, how I loved the music she was playing, and how I just couldn't believe I was here having a facial. Trish finally cut me off in mid-sentence and told me that she didn't talk during sessions and neither should I. I should just focus on relaxing and meditating. Feeling chastised, I wanted to know exactly what Trish was up to if she didn't want to talk. I couldn't see as my eyes were covered with a wonderful eye blinder that smelled, oddly enough, like fresh roasted nuts.

Instead of meditating, my mind wandered. The motions of her hands and the products she was slathering on my face reminded me of college and a Stage Makeup 101 class I took during a one-month session called May Term at Transylvania University (yes, it's a real school). In that class, we painstakingly made plaster casts of our own faces. It involved sticking straws in your nostrils while your classmates poured some mixture of concrete and Plaster of Paris completely over your entire head, then sitting perfectly still while it set. Once set, you could remove it, and fill it with another plaster mixture. When that hardened, you had an exact replica of your head. As I thought of this, I could not believe that I had (a) trusted my friend Elizabeth, who was the least responsible person I knew at school, to stick straws in my nose then cover me in plaster, and (b) not used that plaster cast of my 20-year old self as art in my current 40-year old self's own home. I made a mental note to find that head as soon as I got home. In another exercise in Stage Makeup, we took head shots of ourselves and then sectioned the pictures into four quadrants. It was in this exercise that my perfection was revealed. My makeup professor was amazed, and told me I had the most symmetrical face she had ever seen. She had never seen a face that was so perfectly even on all sides. It was without a doubt, one of my proudest moments at Transylvania University, and it is a compliment on which I have since always hung my hat—I have a perfectly proportional face!

Of course, I now began to wonder if Trish was noticing how symmetrically perfect my face was as she worked on it. Was she thinking to herself she needed to try and snap some photos of this perfectly symmetrical face for training purposes? Maybe she was considering asking me if I would be willing to serve as a model when she tutored some of the up-and-coming aestheticians at the spa. I decided I would be gracious and allow Trish the use of my face.

These thoughts settled my nerves, and I allowed my perfect face to receive its treatment. As she dabbed and smeared creams and lotions on to my face, I wondered if she ever wrote out words on client's faces with her products during this part of the treatment. No one would ever know. The smells-like-hot-nuts-pack would cover the client's eyes and no one else would be in the room. If I were her, I would at least be tempted to write out my name with some of the lotions before rubbing it into the skin. If I didn't particularly like the client I was working on, I would write "Nerd" or "Snooty" on her cheek. But then, Trish seemed to be a professional, and would never consider such foolishness. Besides, right now I bet she was enamored at the perfect symmetry of the face that was glowing before her.

After an hour, Trish informed me in her whisper she was finished, and I should lay there as long as I wanted, then put my robe on, and meet her outside in the sitting area. I have to admit I was disappointed that the facial was over, but my excitement was just beginning. If a simple facial had been this relaxing, I can't imagine what the hot stones would do for me. While I lay there, half in and half out of consciousness, I decided this place, this spa, must have some magic in it. I couldn't have fallen this easily and this fast out of my, "I hate spas," mantra without some extra-sensory help. I reluctantly put on my robe and slippers and meandered into the hall, where Trish, who I had now determined was some sort of fairy with magical powers, gave me some fairy juice—water with cucumber— sat me down in a chair to wait for my next treatment, and slowly flitted away into the ozone.

After a few minutes, Grace, the Hot Stone Fairy, entered and led me to a new room. Knowing the routine, I stripped, covered myself with the sheet and prepared for my massage. I was still uneasy about being touched and rubbed, but I have to admit, my life as I knew it changed the moment the first hot rock was placed on body. In my naivety, I assumed that in this type of massage, the rocks were just heated and placed on your body and that was it. I had no idea they were rolled in oil then massaged into your skin. Had I known Grace would be working over my entire body, including my feet, I would have made sure to clip my toenails before arrival. Since I didn't, I was humiliated I was not properly groomed and felt my overgrown toe nails were long and sharp enough to allow me to climb a tree.

As the Hot Stone Fairy began working the hot stones up and down my back, legs, arms, feet, and hands, I had a religious experience. My previous thoughts of massages were irrelevant. I wouldn't have cared if my toe nails were actual talons. It was sensational, and it was far too pleasurable to keep my mouth closed. I think I counted three unintentional moans during the treatment, and at two different moments, I was ready to speak in tongues with my eyes rolled back in my head. I didn't care who heard it.

When Grace made her way to my shoulders and neck with the hot stones and her magic fingers, all she would have had to whisper is, "Tell me where the Stewart family treasure of gold is buried," and I would have gladly told her. It would have been in a foreign tongue, though, because I was unable to speak English at the time, and barely able to hold in my spittle. (Side note: there is no actual buried Stewart family treasure of gold, I repeat, there is no actual buried Stewart family treasure of gold.)

At the end of the hour and half long treatment, I was a mere pile of skin and bones. I had never been more relaxed in my entire life. Why, oh why, did I think I would not like this? This was NOTHING at all like being mashed up against sweaty people in a high school hallway or crammed into a Subway car in 90-degree heat trying to balance yourself by grasping an overhead handle. This was manna from the Gods. This was true and complete relaxation. I was born again. I was a convert. I wanted more. More of everything: more facials, more stones, more massages, more fairy juice—which was waiting for me just outside in the sitting area.

Grace, the Hot Stone Fairy, told me to gather myself and, when I was ready, put on my robe and slippers and meet her outside. It took a good five minutes before I was sure that I could actually stand. My legs were like jelly. I felt amazing as I headed back to the sitting area to await my final treatment of the day.

Trish, my original fairy, soon came to get me for the Pièce De Résistance, the Green Tea Detoxifying Body Treatment. I was on such a massage high I felt almost drunk. If Trish said we would begin the treatment with my shedding the robe and streaking through the courtyard of the resort, I would have whole-heartedly agreed with her. But again, Trish is a professional and would never say such to me or any other client, but she has that kind of power.

During the first part of the body detox, I was scrubbed down with a stiff brush. My eyes were once again covered by the savory roasted nut scented bag. After I was all scrubbed, Trish proceeded to paint my body with a gooey substance that felt quite lovely. If I am being honest, it sort of felt like a dog was licking me. Even though I didn't actually see, I am fairly sure the Spa Fairies used a paint brush of some sort, and not a real dog.

After I was slathered with the goo, I was covered in hot, steamy towels, and then bound tightly into a cocoon. Trish politely whispered she was leaving me so I could relax while my body de-toxed. I was already so relaxed; I was almost comatose. One sudden flash of worry came to me as Trish left the room. What if last night's pickled bologna had been a terrible mistake? What if the detoxification process resulted in an unpleasant odor? Let's be honest, if anything is going to stink while leaving your pores, it is pickled bologna. But the worry was only a flash. I was so relaxed I couldn't focus on anything for very long. If I had my c-pap machine with me, I would have slept there on the table for thirty-six to forty-eight hours, guaranteed.

In a few minutes, Trish woke me up, and had me shower. In the shower room, I was surprised to see the goo had dried and was a dark blue/black color. I am not sure what I expected, but that was not it. I looked like a rejected member of the Blue Man Group. I was relieved, too, that I smelled no lingering pickled bologna remnants. After showering off the dried goo, I stumbled back to the table where Trish then slathered and massaged my body in a green tea moisturizer. She whispered for me to lie as long as I needed, then put my clothes on, and head out to the sitting room. My day was complete. I was so relaxed and high from this glorious day, I didn't want to get off the table. I immediately began to wonder how long it would take for Trish to come check on me if I just didn't move. She HAD said to take as long as I needed.

I finally gathered my strength, put my street clothes back on, said my thank yous and goodbyes to the Spa Fairies and staggered out the door. I am not sure how I made it back to our cottage, which was on the other end of the resort, but the next thing I remember was waking from a nap wrapped in the lush linens of our bed in our bedroom.

Andy assured me I had a massage high, and I told him I was now hooked on the junk. I immediately sent a text to Donna to tell her to schedule a spa day for us. I was already jonesing for my next hit.

So there you have it. I was wrong. Wrong, wrong, wrong. I realized it isn't so much that I do not like to be touched. I do, indeed, like it, as long as you are a professional with hot oil, roasted-nut smelling eye covers, strong hands, and charge by the hour. Wait. What? Well, you get my point.

Arm Day at the Gym

I have a love-hate relationship with working out. I love the idea of pushing yourself to the limit and reaping benefits like those attitude-adjusting levels of endorphins, a chiseled chest and washboard abs, the knowledge your body—your personal machine—is running clean and at peak levels that will keep you healthy and viable long into your golden years. The problem is I hate to sweat. And working out takes a lot of effort. And desire. And dedication. I like to think of myself as care-free and not overly aggressive or vigilant. I call this being laid back; others call it lazy. Whatever. All I know is I just don't like to exercise.

The only thing preventing me from becoming a man so fat he is offered his own reality show on TLC, or seen on the evening news being saved from his bed with the help of a forklift and Richard Simmons, is my vanity. I have long suspected underneath my layer(s) of baby fat is the body and face of Tom Cruise. We already nearly have the same color hair and eyes (honestly, I am not sure what color his eyes are, but they make colored contacts so it's no big deal if I need to change mine), and we both have big personalities.

In order to achieve this movie-star handsome persona waiting to be uncovered, I have worked out in seemingly every gym in the southern United States. I have tried all different types of facilities—the multi-level mega gym with neon and leotards everywhere to the small hometown gym that is more or less a guy's garage. Once, I even tried a karate lesson gym, but discovered I bruise like a ripened peach, and disliked pain even more than sweat.

A particular gym in Ormond Beach, Florida, however, struck my eye. It seemed the type of place one could really find his inner

Tom Cruise, a place where the support staff would encourage my Tom to come out and show the world his true self. EZ-Bodee is an upscale, full-service gym that can give you a workout you will remember for days. They have personal nutritionists who consult with you about your diet, and they have personal trainers who hold your hand and kick your butt every time you come in the place. I am drawn to fancy places like a moth to a flame, and EZ-Bodee was both exclusive and successful, therefore assuring my membership. I was sure that with all this help and personal attention (have I mentioned how much I love attention?), I would have a beach-ready body by swimsuit season. Of course, living in Florida, a place where it's always swimsuit season, gave me absolutely no timeframe, so I couldn't fail.

On my first workout visit, the first thing I notice about the gym is that while the trainers and nutritionists are friendly, the other members of the Club are a little stand-offish. Not ever being one to shy away from fitting in, I decide, along with unleashing my inner TC, I would win them all over within a couple of weeks. Soon, my fellow EZ-Bodeers would all rise up from whatever weight machine the trainers had them on and yell, "Hey Keith!" when I walked into the facility. I just have a good feeling about this place.

**

I am two weeks into the program and can see no visible difference in my body when I examine it for changes in the bathroom mirror at work. I think I hear a muffled Tom Cruise-ish voice murmur to me, "Keep going," so I rush and finish up for the day and head straight from the office to my appointment with the trainer. When I walked onto the floor, I look around expectedly, but no one raised up from their workout to say hi. That was ok. All in due time. They would like me eventually.

I head to the locker room to change clothes and get ready to sweat. While there, I decide with all the pushing, pulling, and straining I was preparing to do, I should go ahead and prepare my body as well, if you know what I mean. There is no need being even more uncomfortable than you already are when bent over a machine and lifting a weight with the back of your calves.

I head to the first stall and do my business. Before I go any further, let me assure you I was raised right, and I courtesy flush several times while conducting business in public. As I hop up, refreshed and ready to go, the automatic toilet flusher begins a final flush. My life slowly turns into slow motion as the key to my brand-new car falls out of my workout shorts and into the toilet bowl. "Nooooo!" I yell.

Then I do it.

I go in after it.

The industrial flush was sucking the water out at a near bionic rate and along with it the keys to my new car. While this process probably took only a second or two, it seemed like an eternity.

The good news is I was fast enough. My freakishly tiny hands finally came in useful for something, and I was able to slide my hand all the way into that hole in the toilet bowl that leads to who knows where. I grabbed hold of the keyring just as it entered that dark cave, my hand jammed into the opening. The bad news is when I gripped the key to save it, I had to make a fist, and in fist position, my tiny hand was too big to come out of the toilet hole.

So, here I am on my hands and knees in front of the toilet with my arm in the water, hand in the hole. If I let go, I will lose my key, and if I don't, I can't get my hand out. Panic quickly ensues. I fight the urge to scream, then I fight the urge to cry. I try opening the stall door, but in the awkward position I was in, there was no way to do it. I consider yelling for help, but no, this was a fancy gym, and I couldn't be seen this way if I ever wanted to fit in here. Tom Cruise would never let himself be caught on his hands and knees in the stall of a men's room.

In a minute or so, someone comes in to use the restroom. I hear him sidle up to one of the urinals beside the stall. I swallow all pride and say, "Hello? Hi." My greeting is ignored, so I tried again, "Hello? Hi."

A gruff, "Yeah?" responds.

I am so happy and relieved and nervous that this man has acknowledged me that I just spill all the beans and ramble out the entire story to him. "Oh, thank goodness! Yes! Sir, I was in here using the bathroom, and I dropped my car key into the toilet while it was flushing, and I went in after it, and well now, I have gotten my arm stuck in the toilet."

I am so relieved. I would be saved after all. But instead of a response, I hear nothing. Nada. Visions of the Ormond Beach Fire and Rescue Department cutting me out of this porcelain throne start clouding my sight. I start in again, in case he didn't catch it all the first time, saying exactly the same thing but an octave higher and with more worry in my voice. The gruff voice cuts me off and says, "I heard you. What do you want me to do? Tell someone?"

"Nooo!" I said with a little too much force. "I don't want to be seen this way by anyone. Not in this gym!" I tell him I want him to help me get my arm out. Apparently, I say it with such conviction he is afraid to say no. Either that, or he now thinks he is a victim on a hidden camera prank show.

He walks over to the stall and tries to push the door open. I explain to him it is locked and because I am on my knees and turned the wrong way, I can't get in a position to unlock it. In my panicked state, I instruct this stranger his only option is climbing over into my stall from the neighboring one.

After taking a deep breath I hear the gruffy man enter the stall next door. Suddenly, I hear him grunt and stand on his toilet and look over at the scene in my stall. I don't think he was totally convinced I was being truthful with him until he saw for himself. "I'll be damned," he says, then flings one leg over the top of the divider wall between us.

"Oh man, thank you so much. Thank you," I praised.

"Yeah, let's just get this over."

We then work like two men skilled in service of saving brand-new GMC Envoy keys from the depths of a bathroom toilet. Our plan is brilliant, yet messy. He continually flushes the commode, while I use the water as lubricant to free my fist from the hole. Within 10 or so flushes, my arm is finally freed. The key is saved!

I stumble to my feet, so happy to be out of the bathroom prison, I am laughing and nearly crying. "Thanks!" I say, and although we are still in the stall together, I think a hug is appropriate, but as I go in for the contact, the gruffy man tears open the stall door and walks out.

"Yep," he said. Then he was gone, just like Batman.

I need to sit in the bathroom floor for a minute and collect myself. I am soaking wet from top to bottom from the splattering of the flushed water, and large purple and blue bruises are beginning to form on my forearm. Suddenly, the horror of it all hits me square in the face, and I decide there is no coming back from this. Not at this place. I will never fit in at this snotty gym with its big, powerful self-flushing toilets. I refuse to be known as "Bathroom Boy" or "Toilet Grabber." Inner Tom Cruise will have to wait another day to emerge. I sling my gym bag over my shoulder, hold my head high, and march out of the restroom and through the main floor of the gym. My wet shoes make squishy noises all the way to my new car with my key in my bruised and swelling hand.

As I discover that my soaked, remote car door opener no longer works, I glance across the parking lot to a new Gold's gym being built across the street. Lucky me! Maybe my inner Tom Cruise is over there.

Great Balls of Fire

Last evening, I made red beans and rice for dinner. Andy and I love hot and spicy food. We've never met a pepper or a hot sauce we didn't like. For a kick, I added a fresh jalapeno from my garden to the pot of beans and rice. I de-seeded, sliced, diced, and chopped the dark green beauty I grew with my very hands. I'm no boob. I watch the Food Network. I know it can be dangerous to wipe your eyes or nose with jalapeno-y fingers. I was very careful to thoroughly wash my hands after handling the pepper.

Dinner happened, and it was good, which is always a bit of a relief and surprise when it is my night to cook. A regular evening ensued—dishes were cleared and the kitchen was cleaned. We settled in our matching faux-leather recliners and watched A DVR-ed episode of American Horror Story. All was well.

After watching the show, Andy noticed it was 9:00 p.m, nearly past his bedtime. He hopped up to brush his teeth and settle in for the night. He is one of those early to bed, early to rise ~~freaks~~ people. This left me as the only person awake in the house. The best time of the day. Not that I don't love spending time with Andy, I do. But those of you who live with someone know what a treat it is when you are finally alone in your own home. It's like the feeling you have when you get a good haircut. You just want to smile and know all is good in the world.

On top of being alone, my kitchen was clean, and there was no laundry to be done. I had no lingering chores needing to be finished. I had brought home no work from the office, and I had no email to check. Perhaps most importantly, I had sole control of the television remote control. I was in heaven.

Because I have a Y chromosome, the first thing I did was strip down to my underwear. It's a fact that in order to be truly comfortable, the most clothing a man can wear is a loose-fitting pair of underwear. I stretched out on the couch, and began clicking through the hundreds of channels the satellite dish strapped to our roof sends to our over-sized television. I was ready for a good evening of bad television.

The next thing I did may seem odd to some women reading this. Maybe not. If you have lived with any man—a brother, son, father, husband, boyfriend—you will understand. I know all the men reading will relate. As my mind started chilling out and my body began relaxing, I stuck my hand into the front of my underwear. Not with any crude intention, mind you, I was just holding my stuff. This is a primal, subconscious need every man has, this need to be in physical contact with his member. I don't know why, but when the male mind is cleared and drifting away, holding our penis helps anchor us. By the way, if you are male and you say you don't do this, you are lying. I know it, you know it, and now everyone else knows it, liar.

After five minutes or so of my bliss, I began feeling a strange sensation in my nether region. I removed my hand, thinking this would somehow fix it. It didn't. The strange sensation quickly developed into a full-on warmth. The warmth then progressed to just plain hot. Hot soon became hot as fire. Lying on my couch, I began to panic. Of all my body parts, this one was probably the most sensitive, certainly the most spoiled. I didn't want to lose it to fire. It finally occurred to me that although I *thought* I had thoroughly washed my hands after handling the jalapeno, some residue apparently remained on my digits. I had now pepper-poisoned my penis. I yelled for Andy, but he was fast asleep and couldn't be bothered, so I did what any Southern boy would do—asked mom for help.

Since getting an iPhone, my mom only communicates by text. My sister and I have a "group text" with her that we keep open so we don't have to repeat ourselves over and over, and we can each have a witness to vouch that my mother has been "kept in the loop" on family matters. Knowing my sister was also in on the text, all hope of privacy and dignity immediately were dissolved.

I texted my situation: "911. I cut up a jalapeno tonight. Washed my hands, but it didn't take. I have touched my bird, and I am now dying. Please help."

The first several responses:

"OMG!" from Sis.

"Dear God!" from Mom.

"You have got to be kidding. LMAO!" again from Sis.

Finally, over the shock, my sister told me to stick "it" in something like a bowl of ice. Mom countered, saying milk was a good remedy for spicy things, so she suggested I use a glass of milk.

At this point, the pain was searing, and I was desperate, willing to try anything. I went to the refrigerator and realized I only had almond milk. I decided I had better check with mom to make sure that was OK. Her reply text said, "I am fairly confident it needs to be a true dairy product, so I don't think almond milk would work. Honey, why don't you just buy regular milk? Why do you always have to get the fancy, new-fangled products?" I was secretly a little happy because that shit is expensive, and I would hate to waste a glass even if it was too cool off the red hot poker that was now my penis.

"Do you have any type of true dairy products there? Say, sour cream or cottage cheese?" Sis texted. Mom agreed that would work. I went back to the fridge to discover the only sour cream we had was turned into ranch dip a few days earlier. Although there was plenty, I just couldn't force myself to slather up my member with ranch dip. It seemed very Mickey Rourke in *9 1/2 weeks*, and I didn't like that movie. I also love ranch dip and didn't want to ruin a perfectly good tub of it.

Finally, I told Mom and Sis I would figure it out on my own. I decided just to soak in the bathtub for a while. I then left a cool washcloth covering my junk for a bit longer before bed. After an hour or so, the pain started to subside, and I decided I would live to see another day.

If you take away anything from reading this, please let it be this: hot peppers are mean little hombres. Don't trust them. Watch your back around them. They are clingy. They like to linger. And if you do touch them with your bare hands, do yourself a favor and keep your hands above your waist.

Hot Yoga or How to Self-Administer Your Own Stroke

I am a jaded, jaded man. I have lived long enough with this body of mine to know it will never look the way I want it to look. I always wished it to have very little extra cushioning, and be overloaded with hardness in my arms, legs, shoulders, chest, and torso. But as I have aged, I have lowered the bar on my wants and desires for this temple I call a body. At this point, I would be happy to see my feet when I look down toward them, and I know I have a tattoo somewhere on the front of my hip. I was in my twenties when I got it, and I would like to see it once again before I go to the great workout center in the sky. I don't think that's too much to ask.

I know myself well enough to know, unless a gym is offering all-you-can-eat chicken wings every day, there is no way I will visit it daily. I am extremely lazy and impatient, and looking for a workout to help me lose my excess weight and get me toned quickly and without a lot of effort. So when a few of my friends started telling me about this great new workout they had discovered, I was intrigued. "Tell me more," I eagerly gushed.

"Hot yoga is the best thing ever," my friend Susan said. "It doesn't strain your muscles too much, and you burn *thousands* of calories in just one hour."

"Thousands, you say?" I was intrigued.

"I feel so relaxed and refreshed after hot yoga. I can't believe I lost fifteen pounds in two weeks by simply doing it. I didn't change my eating or drinking habits or anything," gushed Donna, another friend.

"No change in your drinking habits, you say?" My interest was piqued.

These glowing recommendations were all I needed to lose whatever inhibitions my normally grouchy self would impose on a new workout, and head out to the closest Bikram yoga studio. Once there, though, what I discovered was far from a glorified new way to lose weight. What I discovered was the Devil himself has decided to tap into the multi-million-dollar fitness industry with his own special workout. Or perhaps, one of those "scared straight" evangelical preachers is behind it, giving people a little taste of what the third ring of Hell will feel like if they don't change their ways.

For those of you who are fortunate enough to have never been to a Bikram Yoga class, let me explain to you what it is. Bikram Yoga is a supposed beginner's level yoga class with twenty-six stances—or more aptly, pretzel shapes—conducted in bright, fluorescent lighting, at a recommended temperature of 105 degrees. That's right, 105. Degrees. Fahrenheit. 1-0-5.

I fell for my friends' lies, tricks, and ploys hook, line, and sinker. I believed them when they said it would not be bad, and I would feel great afterwards. I believed them when they told me it would balance my chi, and I would live in harmony with the Universe. More importantly, I believed them when they told me it would result in my having a smoking hot body. I even consulted with my friend Jeff, a workout fanatic. He had read all the propaganda about the healthy results of Bikram Yoga, and was more than ready to give it a go with me.

The day of our first yoga class, I starting preparing as soon as I woke up. I drank water incessantly, and I ate proper amounts of protein and carbs at the exact times recommended on the Bikram studio's website. 6:00 p.m. was class time. I met Jeff outside the facility and went to the counter to sign up for the miracle class.

Making sure she first had collected our money, the too-skinny lady at the counter told us some very important rules for the class:

1. No talking inside the actual studio where the yoga will take place.

2. If you cannot do a stance, just stand straight with your arms at your side.

3. If you need to sit down, lay down completely on your back, arms at your side, on your mat.

4. Only drink your water when the instructor says you may have some.

5. You are not allowed to leave the room during the class, which is ninety minutes.

Apparently, these rules are somewhat sacred. In fact, she was so serious and intense giving us the lowdown, I fully expected her to end with, "And the most important rule is do not talk about Bikram yoga," a la Fight Club style.

Jeff went ahead of me into the ~~fire~~ studio to find us two spots while I went to the locker room and changed into my workout clothes. After changing, I confidently opened the door to the studio. What hit me next was a wall of heat that can only be explained by preheating your oven to five hundred degrees and sticking your head inside it. The temperature completely took my breath away. I barely could see. As I tried not to audibly gasp for air, I finally found Jeff who was already on his mat looking dazed and confused. Although he only had been in the room five minutes longer, his shirt was already visibly soaking wet. I unfurled my yoga mat beside his and sat down. Because it was against the rules, we both had an overwhelming urge to talk. Finally giving in, Jeff whispered, "Psst, it sure is hot in here."

"Let's get the Hell out of here," I replied in a voice way above a whisper.

At that moment, the instructor entered the room, and locked the door behind her. She smiled, and began the class. I smiled back, and the nightmare commenced. The very first thing we did was a full body stretch with our hands raised all the way over our heads. Immediately, the wall of mirrors the class was facing showed me I had worn a t-shirt much too short for Bikram yoga. My big, extremely white belly suddenly was on display for all to see as my shirt rose up to the level of a halter top. I altered my stretch to minimize the belly flash, just as the teacher told us now to stretch down to our toes. It didn't take a wall of mirrors to tell me that not only was my shirt not long enough, but also my shorts were ill-fitting. Let's just say if there were a "Plumber's Stance" in yoga, I would have perfectly achieved the position.

I tried to keep up with the different stances and not be self-conscious of how I looked doing them. This became much easier to do as the 105-degree heat and the bright, fluorescent lights and the annoying teacher's voice all kept smashing into me. My last conscious sight was Jeff on his back with his leg in a position that looked like he had been mangled in a car wreck or a skiing accident. He mouthed to me, "I'm sorry. We shouldn't have come."

Then, what I call Bikram Tourette's Syndrome took over my body. I think it was my body's only way of getting through this trauma. I started occasionally yelling out random curse words as I tried to twist and contort my body in ways just not possible. I giggled while illegally grabbing my water. I jumped on one foot while trying to do some "Crouching Tiger, Hidden Dragon" stance. I think I ended just trying to hold the classic position Ralph Macchio made famous in the movie *Karate Kid* when he continued to fight even with a busted ankle. I can't really tell you because I have no real memory of anything other than the heat.

For ninety minutes, I flashed my belly and butt crack to anyone willing to look at it while sweating more than I thought was ever possible. I cussed, prayed, and giggled my way to the end. After the session, Jeff and I sat in the locker room on the cold tile floor. I wanted to cry, and he wanted to throw up. We eventually gathered ourselves, showered and met back outside. I noticed that my left eye seemed to be drooping, and I did not feel better. I didn't feel great or relaxed, and I was pretty sure my chi wasn't up to par either. I began googling "symptoms of stroke" on my phone.

On our way out, the too-skinny perky counter girl informed us that this was a common reaction after the first visit, and that it was, in her exact words, "like 100 percent totally different" after the second class. It would be incredible. In fact, she had taken the class every day for thirty days and felt like a new woman! Words can't describe what I wanted to do to that perky girl. But instead, I foolishly listened to her. If she said it was 100 percent different on Day 2, then who I am to argue with that? She was the expert. Jeff and I decided we would rest one day, then come back for the amazing yoga high promised us after completing Class 2. In happy denial, I drove home, only barely having to hold my drooping right eye open with my hand, more excited for the day off than I was for the next class.

It is said under a lot of trauma your brain will shut down to block the memory of the extreme peril it has experienced. For example, my best friend was hit by a car when we were children, and she doesn't remember a thing about it. She just remembers waking up in a full body cast two days later at the Mary Breckenridge Hospital. Likewise, two days later I had no recollection of what happened to me during my first Bikram yoga class. For some reason, I did not recall yelling curse words, spurting out loud bursts of laughter at inappropriate times or showing my butt crack and fat belly to everyone in my Bikram yoga class. For reasons still unknown to me, I woke up two days later and immediately started drinking water, knowing that I would soon be achieving my promised "yoga high."

I chatted with Jeff mid-morning, and he was a bit reluctant, but willing to try it again. I even went so far as to convince another friend, Anne, to join us for the class. I am ashamed to say I told poor, sweet Anne it really wasn't that bad. I think I may have even told her I knew someone who had done it for thirty straight days—cue the too-skinny counter girl. What was I thinking? I don't know. That's the beauty and mystery of the mind, and also how cults cultivate new members.

During my lunch break at work, I rushed to Target to buy an all-new yoga outfit. I would be ready this time. I knew what to expect. I knew I needed to shop for a really long shirt and loose shorts that would soak up sweat like a sponge. While there, I bought a matching yoga mat. There was no need not to match, even in 105-degree heat. I was out of shape, not a barbarian.

Class time finally rolled around, and I was ready. Jeff was looking a little wary at the thought of going back into the inferno, mumbling something about his equilibrium not being right since the other day. I shielded Anne from Jeff's negativity, and we headed into the room.

As soon as we walked into the studio, I remembered it was the pit of Hades. All the horrid memories of the first class came rushing back. "Ah, Hell," was the only thing I could think.

I decided it best not to make eye contact with Anne. She was looking betrayed and frightened. And hot. Not hot in a good way, but hot as midday August in a Florida parking lot. Anne is a former dancer and in decent shape, but maybe I had oversold this to her. With the "click" of the door being locked, the fluorescent lights came glaring on, and the teacher started her slow torture.

About twenty minutes into the class, I still had not correctly achieved one single stance. Jeff was visibly struggling. He was swaying like a drunk man, and I think I saw a little drool coming out his mouth. Anne, on the other hand, looked comfortable. She had more or less passed out about ten minutes into class and was lying flat on her back with her arms at her side on her mat.

My Bikram Tourette's Syndrome kicked in at about the forty-five-minute stage of class. I was tired of trying this crap and didn't care anymore. I started my cussing and hopping around trying to hold a stance, and my head was hurting. Our teacher at some point had decided that Jeff's name was John, and she was actually calling him out to the class. "Keep up, John," she said, and, "No, no, your other left arm, John." Jeff was so out of it, he responded to being called John and tried in vain to do better. Anne was still comfortably lying on her mat. I could see her chest rising and falling so I knew she was still alive.

With only 15 minutes left in class, "John" had taken as much as he could stand. In a moment of clarity, he gathered his things and starting staggering for the door. I wanted to yell, "John, it is locked! Stop! You'll spoil everyone's chi!" Not that my own behavior had not already ruined the class. John/Jeff stopped just short of the door and plopped down in a fetal position. Anne was still comfortable on her mat, dreaming away.

At the end of the class we woke Anne, and I helped Jeff back to the locker room. We had made it, but where the heck was my yoga high? I felt like I had been hit by a bus. While getting ready to leave, I looked in the mirror, and confirmed it. My right eye was drooping, again. Even more tonight than the previous class. I was pretty sure I had suffered a stroke.

The three of us sat outside in the cool evening air for a bit after we changed our clothes. Anne was fresh as a daisy, feeling great, and said her skin felt remarkably smooth from her sauna nap. Jeff had a worn, beaten-down look to him. I looked like a person who had just suffered a stroke, and should be in the emergency room.

Jeff immediately said he had to work late the rest of the week and all of next week, and therefore not available for class at all. Anne wondered if she would ever get to sleep that night because of her ninety-minute nap. I worried my drooped eye would not bounce back and I would look abnormal for the rest of my life. In the end, we three decided each to go our own way and, just like the Fight Club, never speak of this incident again.

Gloom, Despair, and Agony on Me

By all accounts I should be as miserable as a centipede with athlete's foot. The county I live in falls within the fifth congressional district of Kentucky, and was recently ranked in a government study as the Unhappiest District in the United States. The *New York Times* recently reported that the actual county I live in ranks as the third hardest place to live in the United States. This really isn't the big news story the local Chamber of Commerce was hoping for in order to increase tourism in the area, and I think it pretty much puts an end to the old idiom, "There's no such thing as bad press."

As a white man living here, my life expectancy is only sixty-nine-and-a-half years old, a full seven years less than my fellow white men living elsewhere in our country. Seeing the glass as half full, at least I will be put out of my misery before the bleak, desperate unhappiness of this place grips my heart like a cold hand and squeezes the grit right out of my proud Appalachian spirit.

But here's the thing—until I read those articles, I didn't think I was unhappy. In fact, I considered my life to be not only satisfactory, but downright blissful. I do admit I occasionally get upset when things don't go my way. Sometimes, while browsing Facebook, I am overcome with the urge to jam certain status updates and posts down an ignorant poster's throat. I even have days when my fists stay clenched so long it takes a glass of bourbon, two ibuprofens, and three episodes of "The Golden Girls" to get the blood flowing again to my fingers. I am fairly certain, though, that most everyone else in America has these moments, not just citizens of Eastern Kentucky (please note I would never condone or actually participate in jamming a Facebook status down someone's throat, because that would be crazy, and my people aren't ranked among the craziest in the country, just the saddest. I am pretty sure California holds the title for the craziest people.)

The study whose results tell the world I am among the unhappiest people in the country analyzed areas like physical health, emotional health, and healthy behavior. After examining the specifics of each item tested, then comparing it to my own life, an apprehensive shiver crept down my back. A sudden, inexplicable chill covered my bones. I realized that, indeed, the government was correct—I was engulfed in unhappiness and despair and never even knew it.

I am at the age where it takes longer for me to get rested than it does for me to get tired, but I never considered myself over-the-hill at forty-one. Now, this study tells me I realistically only have twenty-six years left on this planet if I continue living in my hometown. What? I believed myself to be in relatively good physical health. Sure I take a pill for blood pressure, another for cholesterol, one for heartburn, and snuggle up in bed each night attached to a sleep apnea machine. I just assumed that all forty-one year olds did the same thing; little did I know it was only the citizens of District Five.

It really isn't entirely my fault I am on so much medication. My doctor is primarily to blame. You see, as soon as you turn forty, doctors stop trying to cure you of anything. Instead, they give you a sympathetic smile, shake their heads, and tell you they can treat your symptoms. I am sure there is a cure to everything I take a pill for, but because of my advanced age and impending death in just two and half decades, the cost-benefit analysis does not result in favor of my receiving it. Instead, I shuffle to the pharmacy each month, pick up my bag of Diovan, Crestor, Nexium, and whatever other designer drug Anthem Insurance will pay for, and head home to fill up my purple pill keeper box that has two bins for each day—my a.m. allotment and my p.m. allotment.

Even dermatologists are no help to the over forty set. I recently went for a visit to have these small bumps on my ankle and foot checked out. They weren't necessarily "rashy," but they would not go away, and more importantly, they would not tan, leaving my browned feet and ankles looking somewhat polka-dotted. As I tried to explain this to the doctor, she placed her hand on my shoulder, and asked if I really wanted to get rid of them. "Of course I do. I just told you, they don't tan," I said.

"Then find a machine and go back in time twenty years because those come with age and there is nothing that can be done about them," she answered. I wanted to ask her if I were a foot model or a thirty-year old would there be something she could do to eradicate the bumps. But one look at my foot with its hard, cracked tortoise shell-like heel and neglected toe nails told the truth—I was past my prime, past the age of it being cost effective to heal. The best I could hope for was some moisturizing salve or perhaps a Ped-Egg to shave down the layers of hardened, old man heel skin.

My emotional health is also controlled by medications that allow me to be a functioning and productive citizen. Again, I always assumed everyone who lived in this messed up country did the same thing. If not, how did Prozac and Paxil become the darlings of the pharmaceutical world? Don't we all want to experience joy, laughter, and be treated with respect? Don't we all have anxiety, worries, and crazy family members who you swear will show up as guests on the "Jerry Springer Show" during sweeps week? Don't we all stress over paying our bills, cleaning our homes, walking our dogs, and making our husbands, wives, and partners understand that they are wrong and we are right? And what about Republicans? Surely these strange people have emotional health issues. You simply cannot convince me that people in other areas of the country deal with these day-to-day struggles un-medicated, with the exception of NASCAR fans. Those people are nuts.

I have tried coping mechanisms other than medication. I was too out of shape and stiff for yoga to help me. Meditation always ended in my napping the afternoon away, which does not go over well when you work at a desk in an open office with no partitions. Organized religion only left me with more questions than answers. After trying several other options and finding no one single thing that seemed to maintain or bolster my emotional health, I tossed all the ideas into the processor of my confused mind and pressed

"Blend." The result—medication, my only option in achieving a healthy emotional state. Again, I never dreamed it was just us folks in Appalachia who did this. Who knew?

The entire healthy behavior section of these studies is troublesome. It gives "happy points" to people who have healthy lifestyles. It assumes if one counts his calories, exercises daily, and doesn't smoke or drink alcohol, he is somehow happier than the rest of us. Are you kidding me? Have you seen most marathon or distance runners in the Olympics? They look emaciated and as brittle as a frozen corn cob. One harsh flu season could take them out completely. I have tried to live the "healthy" lifestyle. I ate a grand total of fifty grams of carbohydrates from 1999-2003. I drank low-calorie beer. Low. Calorie. Beer. I woke up at five-thirty each morning to go to the gym. I was miserable—miserable and hungry. If the rest of the country is living this way, then I formally request the citizens of U.S. Congressional District Five build a wall to separate ourselves from the rest of the country. We could stock it with BBQ potato chips, Little Debbie Snack Cakes, and Coca-Cola. You know, food that isn't being eaten anywhere else but here.

In fact, if I have one of the unhappier existences in this country, then most of America is damn lucky. You people must be so happy you are laughing and singing and being nice to each other all the time! As for poor old sad me, you can find me at the pharmacy waiting for my prescriptions to be filled, eating a Little Debbie Oatmeal Cake, and wagging my tail like a dog with a new chew toy.

One Shade of Grey

The fact I am aging has not escaped me. I can see it happening. I can feel it happening. Heck, I can even hear it happening.

Clearly, there are a few lines at the side of my eyes when I smile or laugh. There are also some creases in my forehead when I look surprised or sneeze or do nothing at all. All of that can easily be wiped away by my little friend, named Botox, when I feel the wrinkles have crossed a line (no pun intended).

My hands are beginning to look like those of a middle-aged accountant's hands. Two "age marks" have started forming there—splotchy, unsightly dots—while at the same time, the skin seems to have loosened up considerably. My feet have hardened into two unbreakable paddles covered in leather so rough, they can cut you. But, these are issues a laser treatment or two can fix in a jiffy.

My body now aches to warn of impending rain storms or to tell me things such as its refusal to function the next day if made to sleep on anything other than a Temper-Pedic® mattress. Sometimes it hurts for no apparent reason at all, just because it's cranky. All the small injuries I compiled during my years playing tennis has led my body to betray me with fused bones, throbbing joints, and swollen tendons. Again, this is something I expected would happen, and, as any budding old fart would, I sort of like being able to say, "My ankle is killing me, that means it is going to storm tonight."

My knees, elbows, ankles, hips, and neck all crack and pop incessantly. Night and day. 24/7. If some part of me isn't popping or snapping with each step I have taken in the past year, I haven't witnessed it. At this point, I have a regular routine I perform on myself to make sure all my joints and limbs, and any other movable part on my body, can pop before bed.

I have developed the very annoying habit of grunting, "OH!" each time I raise up from a sitting position. I realize all this snap, crackle, and popping probably has a lot to do with being overweight, and because being overweight is not the subject being discussed, I will gloss over it. (See how easy it is to ignore weight-related issues!)

As you can see, I have a pretty healthy grasp on the fact that I am now middle-aged. I gladly acknowledge all the above-mentioned conditions. I fully realize I can no longer eat a pizza at 1:00 a.m. without dire consequences. My idea of "going out" now involves being in bed asleep by midnight. But, nothing, and I mean nothing, could prepare me for what I saw as I showered this morning.

A grey hair. A grey hair DOWN THERE!!

WHAT THE HELL?! No one ever mentioned hair in that area greyed. EVER!

My hair (on my head) started going pre-maturely grey when I was 16 years old, so I am no stranger to hair dye. My chest hair started greying about five years ago—and I have seen many men with grey chest hair—so that was no surprise. But this, this was a horse of a different color (pun intended that time). At first, I thought it was an errant chest hair that had just fallen and drifted down in the area where the "love hair" lives. Then I realized I was wrong, and it was attached to my person. I was paralyzed in the shower. I couldn't move, let alone breathe. I suddenly felt my life flash before me. How has this happened?!

This is apparently some deep, dark secret that the Aging Lords do not want people to know. I am sure if people realized their pubes were going to grey, there would be a lot more research and exploration for Ponce DeLeon's Fountain of Youth. I, for one, would donate money on a regular basis to fund such a search if it meant never again seeing what I did in the shower this morning. Seriously, WHY AREN'T WE FUNDING THIS?

I know there are hair dyes for men's hair, mustache, and beards. I now wonder if they make a dye for the hair in your special place. Perhaps this could be a new business venture for me?

My morning shower ended like a scene from a Lifetime movie. I hunched down and cried a bit while the warm water poured down over me. I think I may have thrown up a little bit in my mouth. I then pulled myself together and stood up, grunting, "OH!" as my knees popped, grabbed the grey bandit, held my breath, and yanked out the hair from my nether region. If the old wives' tale about pulling out one grey hair and seven growing back in its place is true, then I have a lot to think about this week. One thing is certain, manscaping is in my immediate future.

Return to Sender – The Letter File

Writing letters is a lost art. No one has the time or inclination to sit down at a desk, take out a piece of nice stationary, pick up a favorite pen and write in longhand the events of one's life. Even if you do take on this task, you then have to mail the letter which requires a stamp and a trip to the post office. The letter then takes DAYS to reach the intended recipient, who in the meantime has seen your Facebook posts and Twitter tweets and already knows everything you put in the letter. It's a losing battle unless you are writing to someone who lives on a deserted island and you are the sole provider all outside information. Good luck finding that person.

There are times, however, that I wish letters were still in style. There is something very satisfying about being able to add someone to your "list" of people you need to write a letter to or about in order to exact proper revenge or retaliation for being slighted in some way. A strongly worded text or email just doesn't have the same punch as a true letter.

Letters of apology are also a much more graceful method of showing your remorse to someone than, say, a text saying, "Sry!" If you are anything like me, your texts make you look illiterate anyhow. Each time I think my spell check will automatically change a word to the correct one, it doesn't, and every time I go ahead and change the word in question, spell check changes it to something completely unrelated.

In a perfect world, I would be a letter writer. I would write all types of letters. I would be known far and wide for my communication skills. As I have dreamt about it, I have also concocted letters that I wish I could send. Letters that needed to be sent. Recipients who needed to be educated on what is what. But, alas, after writing them, I always file them away in a desk drawer, waiting for that day when letter writing becomes a fad once again.

Some examples of my Letters Never Sent:

December 4, 2010
Older Gentleman Who Obviously is Not a Juddhead
KFC Yum! Center
Louisville, KY 40202

Dear Older Gentleman Who Obviously is Not a Juddhead,

I want to express my deepest apologies to you for having the unfortunate luck of sitting in Section 3, Row L, Seat 18 last Friday evening at the "Judds: The Final Encore Tour" concert in Louisville, Kentucky. Your luck was unfortunate because I was sitting directly behind you in Section 3, Row M, Seat 18. My fellow Juddhead, I am truly sorry for singing every single word of every single song, almost at the volume of Wynonna herself.

I did not mean to continually bump into the back of your chair. It's just that sometimes my dancing gets a little rambunctious and body parts go places I don't think they necessarily will go. This problem was also accentuated by my adding a few extra pounds to my frame since the last time I really danced, and I was a little unsure of my body's boundaries.

I do feel just terrible about spilling drops, some quite large, of beer down your back and shoulder. I was overly excited and really should have been drinking from a sippie-cup. I know you asked my friend sitting beside me a question, and he ignored you, but I will go ahead and answer you now: No, it was not possible to put the beer down for just a minute. You see the cup served as my very own microphone.

Most importantly, please believe me when I tell you that I had NO IDEA I had somehow turned music on my iPhone and played Abba Gold - The Greatest Hits on a repeat loop for the entire concert in your ear. I do hope you like Australian Supergroups, and they blended with the harmonies of Wynonna and Naomi.

If you really think about it, though, sir, your discomfort is a little bit your own fault. Had you stood up for even one moment of the concert, any and all of the above grievances could have been avoided. I have never understood people who attend concerts and then just sit and quietly watch as if they are watching a movie. Perhaps I am unsophisticated or just plain red behind the collar, but when live music is played in front of me, I like to show my appreciation by whooping and hollering, clapping my hands and, occasionally, dancing. Now that I think about it, this probably is why I was asked not to renew my season tickets to the Lexington Philharmonic.

Also, Mr. Row L Seat 18, if I had not completely lost my mind and had an out-of-body experience when Wynonna started singing "Born to be Blue," your forehead would have never made the jumbotron as the camera captured my most awesome dance moves to one of my all-time favorite songs. I was happy to share the moment with you, even if to the entire crowd at the Yum! Center I looked like a true, crazed Juddhead and you just looked bored. Again, that is your own fault.

In conclusion, Mr. Section 3 Row L Seat 18, I think you should re-evaluate your level of devotion to the Judds. I know that Mama Judd was off-the-hook-crazy and looked like she was not only drugged, but also injected, botoxed, and stretched to the point of no return. Wynonna, however, was so much more self-confident with her mother beside her that her performance was amazing. What more could you want in a concert, Mr. Man?!

Nothing, I tell you. It was perfection.

Next concert, you may want to consider sitting in a safer seat. One that isn't on the main floor, and more importantly, one that isn't near me.

Sincerely,
Keith Stewart

Wynonna Fan of the Month
December 2010

04/03/2011

Rutgers, The State University of New Jersey
57 US Highway 1
New Brunswick, NJ 08901-8554

Dear Rutgers University Graduation Committee,

    I understand how difficult receiving adequate funding for public colleges and universities can be in today's financial climate, and I am sure you are feeling the effects of crunching your numbers and cutting valuable programs or laying off qualified, professional educators in order to balance your budget. The public schools in my home state of Kentucky are facing the same dilemma, and I am not going to lie, those decisions are tough to make and even tougher to enact.

    After reading this week that you paid $32,000 to Nicole Pollizi, or Snooki as she is more commonly known, to come to your campus and lecture your students, I had a brilliant idea. I know you have contracted Toni Morrison to speak at your graduation ceremony this May. I also know that you are paying Ms. Morrison less than the 32k you paid to get the caliber of lecture you received from Snooki. Kudos to your very savvy negotiators, because clearly you made the better deal spending more state taxpayer money on Snooki! I mean, does the Nobel and Pulitzer Prize winning author, Toni Morrison, even have a nickname? I think not. To make matters worse, when asked what she thought about being paid less than Snooki, Ms. Morrison's reply was, "I don't know her...and I don't care." What?! Who in her right mind doesn't know Snooki? Perhaps after writing iconic books, such as *Beloved* and *Song of Solomon*, Ms. Morrison went into seclusion, not watching realty shows on MTV and only talking to other academics or, worse yet, Oprah.

    That being said, it is with great excitement that I present to you my proposal for Rutgers University. Instead of shelling out too much money for lame Toni Morrison, continue the trend you have established and allow me to give your commencement address in May. I will wager a bet the amount of Snooki's fee that Toni Morrison does not know who I am or care about me either, just like Snooki. I am sure that I can continue the in-your-face stupidity and total nonsense that Snooki delivered, and my fee will be very nominal—only $10,000. You can save enough doing this to afford larger television sets in the student lounge for your students to watch episodes of Snooki on Jersey Shore or, better yet, to install some tanning beds and help your students achieve that orangey, artificially tanned "Snooki-look."

I am not on a realty show, but I have been told my dysfunctional family would make an excellent one, so it is probably only a matter of time before MTV, TLC, or the Horror Channel picks us up for a season. You would be getting in on the ground floor of my fame.

Like, Snooki, I also have several nicknames. My favorite is "Shig," which is short for "Shiglyogly. (pronounced Shig-Lee-Ogg-Lee)." If it would help matters, I am more than willing to add and "i," to the end and simply be, "Shigi."

While I do not have long hair, and therefore, will be unable to produce the poof of hair that Snooki seemed so proud of during her lecture to your college students, I have seen the BumpIt infomercial several times. I know how it works, and feel just as qualified to speak to the merits of a hair-mass lumped up on top of one's head.

I understand that some of your students were disappointed that Snooki showed up for her lecture completely sober. With me as your commencement speaker, that is a problem you will not have to worry about at all. I am totally willing to be contractually obligated to be completely shit-faced when I take the podium. This is Rutgers University, and I will respect its graduation ceremony. This probably has been the best six to seven years of your students' lives and they deserve—nay—they demand a drunken commencement speaker. On a side-note, I know there is nothing in Toni Morrison's contract guaranteeing her drunkenness. In fact, I bet the 80 year-old sips tea, not straight Jägermeister like Snooki and me.

I know it will be tough to top the advice Snooki doled out to the audience. Most cannot compete with, "The more you tan, the better you feel," and, "Study hard, but party harder." These are lessons that Snooki undoubtedly learned while attending community college somewhere in New Jersey, but I know that I can dig deep and inspire your students as well. Here are three tidbits that have already popped into my head as I have written this letter:

- A day without sunshine is like, you know, night.
- I owe a lot to my parents, especially my mother and father.
- I say no to drugs, but they don't listen.

Sure, they are not at the level of Snooki, but neither am I asking for as much money as you paid her, and they are darn sure better than anything an 80-year-old woman-with-no-nickname can produce.

I hope you will consider my proposal. If I can provide any further information to prove that my white trashiness is on the same level as Snooki's, please do not hesitate to ask. I will gladly send you my arrest record, personal references, and lists of people who have issued restraining orders against me. I anxiously await your reply.

Sincerely,

Keith Stewart

p.s. I forgot to mention that my family once got into a brawl at a graveside funeral. I bet Toni Morrison's hasn't.
p.p.s. I can also cuss like a sailor, and will willingly do so.

July 13, 2014

Frothington Bernheimer
123 Beach Avenue
Daytona Beach, FL 32114

Dear Frothington,

Congratulations! It is with great pleasure I bestow on you the award for the Worst Blind Date Ever. This is an honor which many have striven for, but few have achieved. Not only are spectacular qualifications needed, but also fortitude, grit and endurance. Tonight you showed all of the above, plus some!

The previous holder of the title, Mr. Jeremy Padsworth, kept the honor for five long years, and few thought his awkward, mismatched outfit two sizes too small, and his self-diagnosed case of Tourette's syndrome could ever be topped. However, when you showed up on a Segway with one of its original wheels replaced with a bicycle tire, I knew you had potential to take his crown.

As you made your way across the busy plaza to meet me at our agreed upon park fountain, I immediately knew the Segway's mismatched tires failed to impart enough speed to derive any wind to cool you from the heat of the July sun. Your clothes were sopping wet with what appeared to be a slicker, slimier sweat than I am used to seeing. And, boy howdy, you do not have to tell me twice you use one of those organic deodorant rocks over products that, say, actually work—like real deodorant. Your smell actually made a couple of children standing in the plaza cry, and that, my friend, is the smell of a champion.

You sealed the deal for the award with your lovely greeting for me, which I imagine you had practiced several times while preparing for our blind date. I can just see you, staring nervously into your bathroom mirror going over your lines while you rolled that rock up under those horrific pits. As I stood and extended my hand, you stopped, looked at me from head to toe, then spun me around and I assume did the same to backside (smooth move, sir, smooth). Spinning me back around to the front, you then said in a voice much louder than necessary, "Shit fire and save the matches! I've got me a live one here! You're a little plump for my normal tastes, but daddy's back is hurting from riding my Hog down here, so a little cushion for the pushin' is just what I need tonight." If ever there were a better opening line for the WBDE Award, I am not aware of it. Bonus points for calling your broken-down Segway a "hog."

As I pulled my keychain mace-dispenser out of my pocket and turned my back to leave you, I allowed myself a smirk and a shiver. I knew I had just encountered a new douche master. It was an honor, similar to being the first murder victim in a horror movie, to meet you.

Again, congratulations! Know your story will live on for many years in the Worst Blind Date Ever Hall of Fame!

Sincerely,

Keith Stewart

The Line Judge

Ladies high school volleyball is the most deceiving game in sports. Unlike basketball or soccer, the girls in high school volleyball tend to wear ribbons and bows in their hair. Many have a demur, calm look about them. They appear just as likely to be seen at the mall with friends as on the hardwood court smacking a ball. But once they start playing, they become some of sports roughest, toughest athletes, showing no mercy as they send balls flying towards opponents' heads at 100 mph. My niece is one of those chameleons, and I love going to watch her play. I am always surprised at the force and ferocity with which those sweet-faced girls hit the ball at each other. The games are basically slug fests, and the team who crams the ball down the other team's throat the most wins.

Last week, I arrived early at the local high school for my niece's game in order to get a good seat down front and at center court. So I am sitting there on the metal bleachers, minding my own business, thinking to myself, "Honestly, when is someone going to invent a better bleacher? One that doesn't leave your rump numb for two hours after sitting on it for half an hour."

Suddenly, my niece's coach is motioning me to come down to the floor. Never good at deciphering signals, I act like I know what her wave means. I laugh, smile, nod my head, and point at my shirt then rub my belly, like I am responding to a baseball coach giving me orders from beside third base. I don't know why I think rubbing my belly is an appropriate response, but it is all I have to offer. The lady sitting beside me finally says, "I think she wants you to go down there." I stop my insane hand gestures and awkwardly walk down to the gym floor.

In high school volleyball, there are two official judges/umpires/referees who are trained, impartial, and paid to call the game. There are also two line judges that the home team provides. These people stand on the court during the game and watch where the ball hits the floor and call it either in or out. Until that night, I always assumed the line judges needed to be responsible members of the sports community. After the coach asks to me to serve as one, I realize they just get anyone off the street to do it. "All you have to do is raise the flag up if the ball is out, and lower your flag if the ball is in," I'm told.

"Easy-peasy-lemon-squeezy," I reply, ignoring the worried looks the coaches and other officials have plastered to their faces.

As I walk out on to the court and look up at all the spectators, I immediately become self-conscious. I know these people have come to watch a volleyball game, but in my mind, suddenly they are all here to watch me call the lines.

My internal conversation with myself as the girls warm up:

"I wish I had shaved this morning. I don't know why I don't just suck it up and shave every day."

"Really? You don't remember you vowed to never again shave daily once you left corporate work?"

"I do, I just don't like having all these people look at me with my salt and pepper whiskers. On some men, it looks good. On me, it just looks wino-ish."

"Well, it's too late now. Suck it up, Bucko." (*I can be so hard on myself.*)

I snap back to reality when a volleyball hits my leg. Some girl from the opposing team smiles and runs over to grab it. I then begin to wonder how much power I have in this position:

"If someone hits me on purpose with the ball, can I throw them out?"

"If I think someone has a bad attitude, can I give them some sort of penalty?"

"Do I have the power to just end the game if I want to do it?"

As the game starts, I am trying to pay close attention, but the glaring eyes of the fifty or so spectators staring at me begin wearing me down. Suddenly, I begin to panic, considering all the bad things that could happen in this game:

"What if my nose itches and I raise my arm up to scratch it and everyone thinks I am calling the ball out when the ball isn't even on my side of the court?"

"Worse yet, what if people don't see me scratch my nose, but think, instead, I am standing there just picking it?"

After the first set, I am over this judging. My concentration falters, my mind begins to wonder, and my feet begin to hurt. I start having more random thoughts and conversations with myself:

"I am really tired just standing here. They should provide us a chair."

"My feet are hurting."

"Dude, you need to get in shape if you are hurting from just standing."

"Although I must say, I AM having to stand with proper posture AND having to suck in my gut because all of these people are watching me. Plus, this floor has no give. If not chairs, they should give the line judges anti-fatigue mats to stand on."

Finally, I have lost all control of my thoughts and of any close calls happening on my side of the court:

"I should have eaten dinner before coming tonight. I am starving."

"I wonder what time I will get home. Will it be too late to cook something? Should I stop somewhere before I go home? Maybe run through a drive-thru? A Dairy Queen Blizzard would be good, but I can't have that for dinner."

"I know I still have half a package of tofu in the refrigerator at home. How old is it? Does tofu go bad?"

At that point, a volleyball goes whizzing by my head, barely missing me. I look up to see it was hit by my niece who was serving from the other side of the court. I can't be sure, but I think she knew I wasn't paying attention and was aiming for me. I gave her the stink eye and held my flag straight up. "Out!" I said with a flourish, making my authority known for one, sad brief moment in time.

I wanted to scream, "Not in my house!" but I didn't. I just kept standing there, but was a little more alert for the rest of the match.

The love of family can make you do things you never considered doing. I had no business on a volleyball court in any official capacity, yet there I was, holding in my gut for five grueling sets all for my niece. Although I am sure they will never ask me again to help, I am glad I was there to be a part of her high school experience for at least one night.

And just so you know, tofu does go bad. Really bad.

My Future is So Bright, I Have to Wear Shades

Summer in Kentucky can be a brutal thing. The humidity level mixed with high temperatures make being outside similar to walking around in a sauna. However, in each summer there is always a day here and there that the mugginess and heat take a break and give us Kentuckians a glorious, sun-filled perfect day. When these days happen, you have to savor it. At the very least, it requires some al fresco dining, if not taking the entire day off from work.

Working for Corporate America, I was never allowed to take such delightful days for myself. I was expected to spend eight to ten hours in my windowless office explaining to my superiors why my department was over or under budget that particular week.

On one such day, after three phone conferences and two meetings, I decided I'd had enough of the fluorescent lighting of my cube and needed a dose of real, actual sunlight. I broke all the unspoken rules of the office and instead of ordering lunch from some place that would deliver to me, I took a lunch break and went outside the building. It was crazy and reckless of me, but my department was only weeks away from yet another restructuring, and I was probably a short-timer at this job anyway.

I grabbed my keys, and reached in my bag for my new sunglasses. I had just purchased the new Ray-Bans, and was quite proud of them. Being the cool guy I am, I went ahead put my sunglasses on inside my window-less office, and walked through the hallway and lobby wearing them. Only very few people can pull that look off, and I was sure I was one of them. I said hello to a few co-workers as I passed, and then went by the security desk at the entrance of the building. For some unknown reason, I had a need for the security guys to like me, and felt obligated to speak to them every time I came and went from the building. Most of the time, they didn't respond. On this particular day, ready to enjoy the sun in my cool shades, I said, "Hey guys! Great day out, isn't it?" All three fellas gave me a look like I was speaking a foreign language. But oh well, as I said, they rarely respond, so I went on my merry way.

Crossing the parking lot on the way to my car, I thought the sun seemed *really* bright. I also started feeling a bit ill. I chalked my dizziness up to being unaccustomed to seeing the sun at this hour, and having skin that's a pasty chalk-white, a color that only accountants and Canadians can achieve. I shrugged it off, hopped into my car, rolled back the sun roof, and headed to the closest drive-thru I could find. I was taking a lunch break, but I wasn't committing career suicide. I was taking the lunch back to the windowless office to eat it.

As I pulled into the McDonalds drive-thru, I was so sick I could barely read the menu board. My head was really pounding, and I felt extremely dizzy. Luckily, I don't really need a menu board to order at Mickey D's. I know the menu by heart. I ordered my combo, and drove up to the window to pay. I noticed the lady taking my money looked at me very oddly. I thought to myself I really must be sick if even the McDonalds worker noticed. I navigated my car back to work feeling worse and worse with dizziness and nausea. As I came back inside through security, I was sweating and clutching my McDonald's value meal close to me. I managed a meek hello to the security boys. They didn't respond, but one did drop his jaw a little. I kept walking toward my office and thought, "Man, I must look as bad as I feel. Something is definitely wrong with me. Am I having a stroke? Do I taste copper?"

I made it back to my office, tossed my keys and sunglasses in my bag, and lay my head on my desk for a bit. I called my boss and told her I was feeling very dizzy and disoriented, and I may go home early. But after a few minutes in my office, I started feeling fine again. I ate lunch, and muddled through the rest of the day. I felt so much better, I even won three games of Free Cell on my computer that afternoon and that takes a lot of concentration.

At day's end, I pulled out my cool-guy sunglasses and put them on to make my exit. On my way out, I decided to stop by the restroom. While there, I looked in the mirror to check my level of hipness.

I was stunned.

Mortified.

I was missing the entire left lens of my cool-guy sunglasses. I had been walking around the office, talking to co-workers, driving, chatting up the Mickey D's drive-thru lady, and hanging with my posse and the security fellas, all while wearing sunglasses that were tinted black on the right eye and completely empty of lens on the left eye. I stared at myself for a long time, then started laughing hysterically. It was one of those laughs you just can't stop once it starts. I wasn't having a stroke at all.

I was just a complete and total nerd.

No wonder our company did not like the accountants to leave the building for lunch. It was for our own safety more than for corporate profits, and who could argue with that logic?

Things That Should Be Illegal but Aren't

I love the strange and bizarre laws states have enacted over the years. Most of these ordinances are no longer, if they ever were, truly enforced. In Hazard, Kentucky, for example, if the authorities arrested unmarried couples in places of entertainment who went off by themselves out of public view (against the law), the jailhouse would be full every time the Hillbilly Palace Lounge offered twenty-five cent wings or one-dollar Bud long necks.

For some laws, it is probably for the best we don't know why they were enacted. I just don't want to know why any Kentucky nudist colony must make itself available to the local sheriff for inspection at any time. What is the sheriff looking for? It makes me shudder to think.

A new trend in irrelevant law-making are local ordinances making it against the law to wear pants so saggy they don't fully cover your rear end. In one locality they are so thorough, they specifically include the measurements for the borderline of low hanging britches. Anything, "more than three inches below the top of the hips (crest of the ilium)," can land you in the Big House.

Don't get me wrong. I hate looking at fellas—and let's face it, it is guys who rock this look—with their butt hanging out for no reason. It just makes the wearer look stupid. Like he isn't smart enough to pull up his damn pants. However, if we are going to fine people for being fashion disasters, we should start with Cee Lo Green or Courtney Love.

Since we are talking about such a civic-minded subject as law making, I would like to propose the following list of things I think should be illegal. I think they stand just as good a chance as the Low Pants Law. Quite frankly, I think they make more sense, too.

THINGS KEITH THINKS SHOULD BE ILLEGAL

- ### *Serving Fajitas in Cast Iron Skillets Heated to the Temperature "2nd Ring of Hell"*

C'mon, is that really necessary? Really? Fajitas are one of the healthier things you can order at a Mexican (or any) restaurant. We are basically talking about some grilled meat and vegetables. Perfect, right? You don't have to worry about fattening cheese, sour cream, or heavy sauces. If you are watching your carbs, you can skip the tortillas and, boom, you are set.

What you DO have to worry about, though, is the loss of your dignity as the server makes a production of running out of the kitchen with a platter of billowing smoke and food sizzling and popping like it's desperately trying to jump off the hot plate. After making the seemingly required lap around the restaurant to ensure everyone sees the smoking mess—and setting off a fire alarm or two—the server, who is wearing industrial oven mitts, sets the platter in front of you and leaves. Sometimes, he will say, "Be careful, that plate is hot." Sometimes not. He should at least leave his set of oven mitts. If he needs them, you probably do too. Furthermore, the smelly food smoke now penetrates every stitch of clothing you are wearing, guaranteeing that you and whoever is lucky enough to be with you, will remember the fajitas long after you leave the restaurant, and that is reason enough to make it illegal.

- ### *Putting the Roll of Toilet Paper So That It Rolls Underhanded.*

There may be some of you who will question why this should be illegal, but it isn't up for debate. The only acceptable way for toilet paper to be placed on a roll dispenser is so it folds over itself and rolls into your waiting hand. The overhanded method is both aesthetically pleasing and functional.

Underhanded rolls have a tendency to unfurl leaving a trail of perfectly good toilet paper all the way to the floor, and honestly, who wants to use tissue that has touched the floor? I don't know how often you clean your bathroom, and I shouldn't be put in the position to have to ask you if it's clean enough to use toilet paper that has unfurled itself to the floor. It is just bad manners.

The only people who use the underhanded toilet paper roll maneuver are sociopaths and future terrorists, which right there explains why it should be illegal.

- ***Strapping Toys & Other Items Down with a Zillion Plastic Ties***

For years, opening a new CD was the bane of my existence. The only reason they no longer give me grief is because I don't buy them anymore. Just as I was beginning to get used to life without the struggle of unwrapping consumer items, the powers-that-be decided to strap in all toys, and most other items that I purchase, with zip ties so securely it takes the muscle of three people and a dog to free them. This is why those powers-that-be need to be arrested.

Is there a legitimate reason that a Barbie should have 32 plastic ties? The answer is clearly no, unless you have purchased a Bondage Barbie, which I am not sure Mattel makes (note to self: see if Mattel makes a Bondage Barbie). I am the first to admit I am not handy with a pocket knife or even scissors for that matter. The pressure of cutting loose a doll or teddy bear without permanently maiming it in the process is too much. I can't stand it. These items could withstand a simultaneous super earthquake and Godzilla attack and remain perfectly arranged in their cardboard box.

With the recent revelation that the National Security Administration invades our privacy more than we realized, perhaps the government is behind this. Maybe they are watching to see who can open up these bad boys with no problem in order to find new Navy SEAL recruits. Unless this is the case, make these plastic ties illegal.

- ***Stickers of Calvin Peeing on Things***

Come on people, have some class. Sure, there are a few folks I really don't like. There are sports teams and towns and states that I don't care for at all. I suppose, deep down, there may be a little part of me that would smile or, perhaps, giggle if I saw something unfortunate happen to one of my enemies. But, am I going to advertise to the universe that I think the best treatment for Nancy Grace or the Duke Blue Devils is for a comic strip character to relieve himself on their heads? No! I will not do it!

When you have one of these stickers on your car, you automatically lose all creditability as a level-headed, sane person. If you are willing to advertise that you get so angry at your opponent or rival you will consider urination as a combat tactic, you already have incriminated yourself as crazy.

- **Saying the following, let alone living by it: "If it's yellow, let it mellow. If it's brown, flush it down."**

OK, I almost puked just typing that. What kind of person does this? I am all for water conservation and living green, but I draw the line at my leaving human waste of any sort mellowing in the toilet bowl. If your home bathroom smells like a Texaco station loo, then you are living wrong. You just are.

- **Couples who share a Facebook account.**

Words can't express how much I detest seeing JohnNSharonJohnson or Tim-And-Jim-Smith on Facebook. Good heavens. Are you so co-dependent that you can't have your own set of online friends? Plus, who are you talking with when they post things? You never know. It is too confusing, and it is stupid. Stop it. The only time this is acceptable is with Siamese twins. If you are Siamese twins and on Facebook, please friend me immediately.

Talk Derby to Me

It is Derby Weekend here in the Bluegrass State. Pretty women are all donning their hats; freshly grown mint is being muddled, mixed with crushed iced, sugar water, and bourbon; country ham is being layered on delicate golden biscuits; and most people are preparing to lose anywhere from one thousand to thousands of dollars in a span of two minutes. Life could not get any better.

This is the weekend to splurge on high-end bourbon, to eat fat-laden and calorie-filled Hot Browns, and to pretend you know all the words to "My Old Kentucky Home." This is the weekend that I always got the most homesick during the years I lived in Florida. On the first Saturday in May, there is no better place to be than Kentucky, rain or shine.

This is also the weekend that all Kentuckians pretend they know something about horses. Being from the mountain region of Kentucky, I was never around a lot of horses growing up, and the ones that were in Leslie County certainly were not thoroughbreds. They were more of your workhorse variety.

When I moved to the rolling hills and pastures of Central Kentucky, I quickly began to learn how to lose money at the track, but still not a lot about the horse itself. This was painfully apparent on a particular Derby Day a few years back.

Lasix is a common drug used in the racing industry. It prevents a horse's lungs from hemorrhaging blood due to the stress of exercise. I am told this is a fairly common "occupational" condition affecting all types of race horses. However, if a horse is using Lasix, it is marked in the racing program with a (L) beside the horse's name for full disclosure, similar to hot dogs being marked with (k) for Kosher. This apparently means something to the handicappers. The (L) not the (k).

I had no knowledge of any of this. The only Lasik I had heard of was the out-patient surgery that miraculously corrected one's vision. I flipped through the racing program trying to decide which horse to bet on before the race. I asked the group of friends I was with, "What does the (L) mean beside the names of some of the horses?"

"That means the horse has had Lasix," says a helpful friend. Then I started noticing almost every horse in the race had an (L) beside its name. I flipped through the program to look at the rest of the day's races. Most every horse racing that day had the (L) mark.

"Wow, all these horses have had Lasik? I had no idea horses were that near-sighted," I announced to my friends. Everyone stared at me. Not noticing, I started wondering out loud, "Has anyone seen a near-sighted horse who was not lucky enough to have the Lasik procedure? Has anyone seen a horse with horse-sized sports goggles strapped on so it could see? Do they manufacture horse contact lenses, and how in the world would you put them in the horse's eyes?"

Everyone still stared at me. Finally, one of my buddies put me out of my misery by calling me an idiot and explaining what Lasix in this situation really meant. "Are you sure you are even from Kentucky?" he ended his explanation as I hung my head in shame.

To answer him, years later, "Yes, I am 100% a Kentuckian." And on this weekend, everyone in the world can be, too. The Derby is a magical time, and even if you don't know Lasik from Lasix, you can choose your favorite horse by any means and root for him or her to win "the greatest two minutes in sports." If you need some help in picking a horse, I offer up this advice:

Keith's Handicapping Tips for Horseracing:

1.   Pick a horse that has a name you like. I like any horse with the word Bird in its name, because it makes me laugh. I don't know why; it just does.

2.   Closely look at the colors of the jockey silks. If you would not look good in that color, avoid that horse.

3.   Watch the NBC profiles of the horses and jockeys on Derby Day. Choose the one who makes you cry the loudest.

4.   Never, ever listen to anyone else's handicapping tips.

Signed, Sealed, Delivered

"Work from home," they said. "It'll be fun," they said.

I always thought working from home would be wonderful. Setting my own schedule, wearing whatever I wanted to the "office,"—basically doing anything I wanted whenever I wanted to do it. How much better could it get? So when the opportunity arose to work from my house as a CPA during tax season, I jumped at the chance.

At first, it was all of those things I just mentioned and more. I enjoyed being able to roll out of bed, stagger to the coffee pot, then get to work. The problem with working this way is very often I would be in my office at 3:30 or 4:00 in the afternoon unshowered, in my underwear and unshaven. The only time I really had to look presentable was when I had to meet a client face-to-face, and I could schedule those meetings in a nice block of time that would minimize having to wear pants.

I will admit I did miss having other people around to talk to during the day. When there is no one to help dissect the previous night's Project Runway episode or to share You Tube videos with all afternoon, the office can get pretty boring. Don't even get me started on how bland the March Madness basketball bracket office pool was for me. However, thanks to the internet, I was able to instant message my way through the tough times. The ability to completely disregard personal hygiene and office clothes outweighed having an office spouse any day.

Living life on the edge like this finally caught up with me on a busy day near the tax filing deadline. I'd spent the day dressed in my red polka-dot boxer shorts, white t-shirt, and striped tube socks.

I had my nose to the grindstone working on a very complicated return. When I heard the mailman outside, I slipped on my sneakers, and ran out to the mailbox to make certain there was nothing in the day's mail that would affect what I was working on. Absentmindedly, I left the sneakers on when I returned inside.

Later that afternoon, I remembered I had some other tax returns that needed to be mailed in order to meet a deadline of that day. I looked at my watch, and realized I only had 30 minutes to get to the post office before it closed.

I rushed, got the returns together, grabbed my keys, wallet, phone, and headed out. I normally looked forward to running errands during this "working from home" period. Many days, this was the only time I saw actual, live people from the outside world, leaving me to seek far too-detailed conversations with the check-out girl at Kroger, the greeter man at Walmart, and the older lady in line behind me at the dry cleaners. This day, however, I was upset that I had forgotten about the returns, and in no mood to go anywhere or participate in idle chitchat.

When I arrived at the post office there was, of course, a long line. I stood there for about twenty-five minutes, rolling my eyes at people who could not get their business done at the counter in what I had deemed a sufficient amount of time. When I was only two people away from being served, I looked down. That is when I realized that I had forgotten to put on actual clothes before leaving the house. I was standing in the post office line in my white t-shirt, red polka-dot boxer shorts, striped tube socks, and sneakers. I had wondered why no one was standing too close to me or meeting my eyes when I tried to get their attention for some "that person is taking too much time" camaraderie. Now, it was obvious—because I was a crazy person.

I then faced the issue of what to do. I had waited so long in line, and I was almost there. On the other hand, I was in my UNDERWEAR in a federal building which I was sure was some sort of felony. I finally decided that the IRS would not care what I was dressed in—or not dressed in for that matter—as long as I mailed the returns. So I waited, walked up to the counter, completed my business, pulled my boxers out of rump (they had ridden up) and proudly left the building, eyes straight forward.

No police cars or federal agents followed me out or contacted me afterwards, although I am likely now on some sort of list of "potential trouble makers" at federal buildings. I decided to go straight back to my office and reconsider my desire to work from home.

I know what you are thinking, and it is true, I did prove myself as a dedicated tax preparer that day. But, with no one back at the office to share this with, what good did it do me?

At least I did not wear bikini shorts or a thong that day.

What Color Is My Parachute? I Don't Even Have a Parachute.

I attended graduate school at Rollins College in Winter Park, Florida. Life was good in Florida. I made amazing friends and learned a great deal, all while taking advantage of the sunshine and warm weather. One thing that followed me to the sunshine state, however, was The Dark Cloud—what I like to call my ever-present bad luck (if you've read any of this book so far, you know about my luck). The Dark Cloud would sometimes raise its ugly head at inopportune moments, causing fits of anxiety that could only be relieved by a nice, slowly-paced trip to Walmart, not necessarily to buy anything—just to browse. I suspect many people may use Walmart to relieve anxiety, to replace a therapy session or, simply, just to feel better about themselves. One visit will confirm that your life is not nearly as bad as you probably thought it was before you entered the *Store That Ate All Other Stores*.

This was in the days before the website www.peopleofwalmart.com existed or I probably could have just stayed home and felt better about myself via my laptop. Peopleofwalmart.com now provides the same therapy, unless, of course, you have seen a picture of yourself on this website, and if that is the case, please, I beg you, call me. I must (a) meet you in person, (b) have someone take a picture of the two of us together, and (c) friend you on Facebook.

Actually, when I visit the peopleofwalmart.com I usually look with one eye open and one eye closed, my body cringed. I know it is just a matter of time before I see someone from my hometown, most likely a member of my own family, on this web site. In fact, you could do an entire site devoted to the Walmarts of Southeastern Kentucky, in particular, the family of Keith Stewart.

The Dark Cloud, however, would also manifest itself in much larger ways than ever could be cured with a little schadenfreude. On occasion—okay a lot of times—relief would require beer. Lots and lots of beer. More often than not, those were after job interviews the Dark Could attended with me.

In MBA school, your final year is spent interviewing with a seemingly endless line of companies anxious to exploit the raw talent of a fresh, newly graduated business person. Companies would come on campus to interview, they would fly potential candidates to the city the business was headquartered in, they would congregate in large convention halls for job fairs. I participated in all types of interviews and in every scenario possible. My only constant through all this was my Cloud.

In my first on-campus interview, I was asked what magazines I read. A fairly routine, average interview question. I went completely blank, then stammered out, "*Time* (which I have never read to this day), *Entrepreneur* (nope, not read it, either), and The *Cat's Pause.*"

The *Cat's Pause*? Did that really come out of my mouth? The *Cat's Pause* is a weekly newspaper that is devoted to the University of Kentucky Wildcats. I HAD read *Cat's Pause* in my childhood. I had even cut out pictures of basketball stars Rick Robey and Kyle Macy and hung them on my wall when I was nine. I had not, however, seen a *Cat's Pause* in twenty years, and why I thought that five men dressed in three-piece suits from the Harris Corporation, a U.S. defense contractor and aeronautical firm, wanted to hear about it was beyond me. At least I had not told them the truth about my magazine reading habits, which included *Entertainment Weekly*, *Mad Magazine* and *The National Enquirer*.

Ironically enough, years later, I would make such fun of Sarah Palin for being tripped up on the same question by Katie Couric. Touché, Ms. Palin, touché.

For another job interview, I was flown to Dallas, Texas, for a position at EDS. Don't ask me what EDS stands for, I still have no idea. Thank goodness that wasn't one of the interview questions. EDS housed all the finalists for the position I was interviewing for in their own company apartment complex. Upon arriving and getting settled into our temporary rooms, an official EDS bus was scheduled to pick us up at our door at 6:00 p.m. for the ride to headquarters for dinner and a meet-and-greet.

I dressed, primped, fluffed, and buffed myself into a shiny, professional looking almost-MBA and waited outside for the bus. As I saw it coming down the street, full of the other finalists, I turned to lock the door of my apartment. I fumbled with the key and dropped it. As I bent down to pick it up and I heard a horrible rip, then felt a slight breeze on my derriere. Yes, my pants had split open from stem to stern. The bus was, at this point, in front of my door waiting, so I ran to its open door, and told the driver and the other four candidates that I would be just a minute, that I needed to go change my pants as I had ripped the ass out of the pair I was currently wearing. I was nothing if not professional.

The day before I was to travel to the nearby Walt Disney Company for an interview, my friends Traci and Jan had driven me to the dry cleaners to pick up my interview suit. "Oh, Mr. Stewart, we've been trying to call you all day," says the dry cleaner, Mr. Chow of Chow's Dry Cleaning. "I am afraid your suit was in the fire."

"THE WHAT?"

"The fire, you don't notice the smoke? The smell?" I had, indeed, noticed both the smoke and the chemical smell all day in the neighborhood, but never dreamed it had been billowing from the one place in the city of Orlando where I had left my only suit to be cleaned for my big interview.

I then lost all control of my professional demeanor. "Let me tell you something, little man. I have a job interview tomorrow at Walt Disney, and I have to have that suit. I am interviewing for a job at the corporate office, not to play Mickey Mouse or to sell turkey legs on Main Street USA. Now, I don't care if you have to go walk through that fire, YOU GO GET MY SUIT."

The man whose primary language was not English politely smiled at me and replied "Yes, we will call you if we find it." Something in me snapped. My language and actions, I am now embarrassed to say, got much worse and I acted out on the dry cleaner. Unflustered, the man kept smiling and nodding, saying, "Tomorrow." Finally, red-faced and defeated, I started back to the car. Traci and Jan had witnessed the entire episode from the front seat. They knew better than to ask any questions until we had driven in silence to the Orlando Ale House and had secured ourselves a pint of beer each.

My suit was retrieved from the fire-filled dry cleaning facility. I wore it to my interview even though it had a charred, smoky smell to it, and believe it or not, I received a job offer from Walt Disney.

So, the Dark Cloud isn't out for blood. It just likes to toy with me, like a cat does to a mouse before going in for the kill. Or maybe it just follows me for kicks and giggles. It knows that no matter what it offers up, I will continue to muddle through, hoping for a sunny tomorrow.

We Had Joy, We Had Fun, We Had Seasons in the Sun

Vacationing is one of my favorite activities. In fact, it may be THE favorite. I love getting away from my familiar surroundings and embarking on a new and exciting adventure. I don't mean a long weekend somewhere, either. I'm talking a full-on, find a sitter for the dogs, place an auto-reply message on the email, no-holds-barred week out of town. I'm not even that picky about where I go for vacation, as long as it isn't camping of any sort. Just get me out of town and in a room with indoor plumbing and air conditioning, and I am happy.

A summer family trip to the beach as a child even brought me my first brush with fame. My family chose the Suntan Motel in Daytona Beach, Florida, to be our home away from home for three consecutive years in the mid-1970s. One afternoon while my sister and I were in the clutches of an intense swim game of Marco Polo with some kids vacationing from Georgia, the motel manager and a photographer walked out to the poolside. With a bullhorn, the manager announced they were going to shoot some pictures to be the new postcards of the Suntan. If anyone did not want to be included, they needed to leave the pool area now. My family decided we would stay as we thought ourselves a nice looking family who may increase the postcard sales for the motel by modeling.

The photographer then began staging the photos. Instead of keeping us together in our actual family, he began pairing people into families who looked more aesthetically pleasing. Since my mother, sister, and I all have dark hair and my dad is the sole blonde in the family, he was sent over to sit with a lady and her daughter who both were of Scandinavian descent.

I was eventually placed in the pool with a man from Canada who the photographer thought most looked like the person who should have been my dad. We were given a beach ball, which was not allowed in the pool under normal circumstances, and told to smile and pass it back and forth.

My mother sat up on her lounge chair and applied Coppertone to my sister's back while a balding older gentleman with a rather large stomach stood above them laughing and reading a magazine in their picture.

My blonde-headed father ended up carrying a picnic basket in one hand, and holding the hand of the tiny Scandinavian girl in the other, while her bikini-clad mother smiled and opened the gate leading to the motel picnic area.

The photographer shot roll after roll of film trying to capture that true family magic that only a beachside Florida vacation—and fake families--can provide. After he had finished, my mom crossed the pool area and made her way to the picnic gate. She grabbed my (real) father by the hand and said, "OK, the photo shoot is over. Let's head out," as she smiled and nodded to dad's (postcard) wife.

We never got to see what the actual postcard for the Suntan Motel in Daytona Beach looked like when it was finished. Two days after the photoshoot, I fell while playing Batman in our motel room, and broke my right arm. We spent the rest of our week in and out of the local hospital and seeing people about casts. But somewhere out there are some great pictures of me, my family, and the people who should have been our family.

****

When I was old enough to vacation without my parents, my best friend, Donna, and I headed to Cancun, Mexico, for a week of fun in the sun. The entire purpose of the trip was to get some sun, drink tropical drinks, and find some good duty-free items to bring home, and that is exactly what we did for the first couple of days. Then I saw the stand of brochures describing all the activities that were possible from our resort. Adhering to Donna's only rule of this vacation—no activity that will mess up her hair or makeup—I carefully scanned the brochures. When I saw the pamphlet touting a guided tour of Mayan pyramids in Chitchen Itza, I knew this was the activity for us. The world famous site was only 120 miles from Cancun, a mere two-hour ride on a luxury tour bus. Once there, we would walk around and look at the amazing pyramids, hop back on the bus, and be back by dinner. No muss or fuss to hair or makeup. It took some cajoling, but I finally convinced Donna it was a once in a lifetime type of trip, and we couldn't let one of the wonders of the ancient world go unseen.

I did not account for road conditions in rural Mexico. One hundred twenty miles in my slice of the world meant the trip would take, at most, a couple of hours. In Mexico, the drive took exactly four hours and twelve minutes. I know because Donna timed it. The word "luxury" has a much looser definition in Mexico than in Kentucky as well. The luxury tour bus may have begun its life in the upper echelons of tour bus hierarchy, but it since had lived a hard life. One that included losing its air-conditioning, the ability to open over half its windows, and the capacity to stop without screeching and sliding a few hundred feet.

We finally made it to the site and our tour guide grabbed our attention by waving a machete over his head. He explained he would use the machete to cut away limbs or *other things* blocking the path to the temple. The hike itself took thirty-seven minutes. Again, I know because Donna timed it.

Finally arriving at the temple, we knew the entire trip was worth it. They were magnificent. I stared in awe. When I saw you could climb up the largest of the pyramids, it was a no-brainer whether or not we were going to do it. Of course we were! I suggested it to Donna. She looked at me with raccoon eyes. Her non-waterproof mascara had smeared from her sweating during the un-air-conditioned bus ride and jungle hike. Her hairspray had not dealt well with the jungle humidity, either. It was sticking up and out in what appeared to be large sections, like a piece of modern art. "Keith Allen, if you think for one second I am climbing up that thing, you have lost your mind," she said. I shook my head in agreement, left her with the camera, and headed out solo.

Leaving Donna on solid ground, I started scaling the seventy-eight-foot-tall pyramid. I was shocked at how steep the steps were, but the trip up was fairly easy, similar to climbing a ladder. When I reached the top, I toured the room inside the pyramid, saw the stone urn where a virgin's human heart was sacrificed on each equinox (that is what they do in the Indiana Jones movies, at least), then decided to climb back down. Fear and panic spread through my body when I saw exactly how steep the steps down were, and exactly how high up I was from the ground. Donna waved and took a couple of pictures of me, but then looked at me. Even from seventy-eight-feet away, I could tell it was an "OK, come on down" look.

I froze. There was no way I could get off the top step. I had neither the balance nor coordination. I then saw the thin rope people were using to balance and scale themselves down the pyramid. I am all for preserving historical landmarks, but at that time, I really did not see anything wrong with a nice metal handrail bolted to the thousand-year-old pyramid, perhaps even an elevator or escalator could be installed. I mean, if you are going to have people climbing up they should be able to safely get down.

Still frozen from fear, I wondered how hard it would be to have the U.S. embassy send in a helicopter to pick me up from atop the pyramid. Most of the tour group had made it down and were making their way back to the bus. Donna had a worried look on her face, and was rifling through her backpack. I hoped she was looking for the embassy phone number, but more than likely, she was just making sure she had all her belongings before heading back to the bus without me. She was not going to be stuck here even if it meant ditching me on top of an ancient pyramid.

Finally, out of the corner of my eye, I saw a lady no less than eighty years old, sitting on the steps and scooting down one step at a time. What a brilliant idea! With age DOES come wisdom! I followed granny's lead and scooted down the pyramid on my butt. I was the last one down, but the bus waited for us, and we happily began our four-hour and twelve-minute ride back to Cancun.

We went back to our original plan for the rest of the week. We spent our days on the beach sipping margaritas, which suited me just fine. My muscles were so sore from the climb up and scoot down, I couldn't have handled any more action anyway, wonder of the world or not.

****

It took a few years, but I finally convinced Donna to take one more vacation with me. I promised nothing out of the ordinary would happen this time, and we wouldn't do anything she didn't want to do. We soon found ourselves, two best friends, in Jamaica. Donna was happy chilling out on the beach and sipping her tropical drinks. I was, too, until I heard about a nearby waterfall that tourists could climb. Guided tours to climb Dunn's River Falls was a "completely safe and nearly effortless walk up one of Jamaica's most beautiful waterfalls," the brochure read. It took a few extra Rum Punches, but I finally had Donna down enough of them to agree to go with me the following day.

The falls were amazing! Three-fourths of the climb was exactly as the brochure promised—safe and nearly effortless. The views were beautiful and natural, other than the locals wading out at each landing offering to braid your hair or sell you a hemp bracelet. We finally reached the hardest part of the climb near the top of the falls. The water was pouring down at full force at this point, and the guide asked our group to line up boy, girl, boy, girl, and to hold hands.

"This chain," said the guide, "will make us stronger than the water plummeting to the surface." I was reminded of the saying "a chain is only as strong as its weakest link." I started looking over the other eleven people in the group, trying to spot the weakest link, but knowing it was me. We started up the final climb, and suddenly, we were actually under the waterfall, with the falls pouring down behind us.

"Wow! This is really cool! I'm so glad we did this!" Donna yelled over the deafening noise of the falls. She was in front and above me, and a German lady was behind and below me. I decided to take one last satisfying look around at the view before continuing the climb, and in so doing, inadvertently pushed my body back from the rock just a bit. I must have pushed back a little too far because I accidentally came into contact with the waterfall.

With the full force of a tsunami, the water rushed down my back and into my swimming trunks, pulling the brightly colored, tropical print shorts all the way down to my ankles. I was panicked and shocked from the jolt of water, and at first didn't notice it. Then I felt an odd body part touching the rock in front of me, a part that should not be exposed. This was just as the lady behind me yelled something in German. I looked down at her, and saw my untanned butt right in her face. I was mooning her.

At this very moment, the line started moving up again. I was stuck, if I lifted my leg, my shorts would come all the way off and be waiting for me at the bottom of the falls, or found and sold by one of the locals trying to earn a buck. I tried to pull my hand away from Donna's. This being the last big push, she was not about to let go of my hand, probably thinking she would need to help pull me up to the finish line. Over the rush of the water I finally yelled, "Let GO!" and jerked my arm away, breaking the human chain, but allowing me to pull my pants up.

After finally making it to the top and explaining to Donna why I had to break the chain, I tried to walk over to the German lady to apologize. When she saw me coming, she said something I couldn't understand, turned, and briskly walked away with her group. I am sure it had something to do with me being an obnoxious American who had given her a moon shot, and perhaps a full Monty, I'm still not sure.

When we arrived home, Donna placed a ban on any travel that included just the two of us. She said she needed a buffer, and would no longer be responsible for getting me home from any foreign location. In fact, I think she may have written a letter to the State Department asking them to revoke my passport. Either way, that was the last vacation Donna ever agreed to go on with me.

It wasn't long after that Andy came into my life, and suddenly I had a built-in vacation partner. Some people like being in long-term relationships for the love, companionship, or security, but for me, having someone who can't refuse to vacation with you is the major benefit. Wish him luck.

You Never Get a Second Shot at a First Impression

Getting a book published has been a goal of mine for a long, long time. I have worked on my writing, attended workshops and studied under some of the brightest authors writing today. I have made it a New Year's resolution every year for many years. My biggest problem in the publishing world? Bad luck and bad first impressions.

"Keith, how can a snappy fella like you make a bad impression, and how bad of an impression can you make?" I know those are the questions many of you are asking yourself at this very moment. The answers are quite easily and stinky bad.

Last year, I attended a Books-in-Progress Conference held in Lexington, Kentucky. The schedule of the three-day event was filled with seminars taught by published authors and very informative panel discussions led by industry editors and publishers. There was also time to share your work with other hopeful writers as well as rub elbows and make connections with people higher on the literary food chain than yourself. All in all, the event was very laid-back and relaxed, but there was a definite buzz of excitement in the air with all the attendees hoping their in-progress work would be discovered and a meteoric rise to the top of the New York Times Best Seller List was imminent.

Of course, being the eternal slacker, I waited until two days before the registration deadline to register. I had not been sure I could take the time off from work, and I didn't have an *actual* book in-progress. I mean, I had a great idea for my book based on the essays and blog that document my strange life, but I didn't yet have it in a book form.

The day of the conference I walked to the registration desk, and was handed my materials. As I started to turn around and search the crowd for my friends, the conference lady said, "Oh, and your appointment is at 11:45."

"Appointment?"

"Yes, with Rita Rosenkranz, the nonfiction literary agent joining us today. You will have fifteen minutes to pitch your book to her."

"Oh!" I said. "Does everyone get this chance or did I win a door prize or something?"

Looking a bit concerned, the lady stated, "Um, no. You paid extra for the fifteen-minute session. You were asked when you registered. Did you not want to do it?"

"No, no, I will do it. I mean, OF COURSE I WILL DO IT," I said way too loudly and then nervously laughed. I was instantly concerned that I had inadvertently signed up for several other things I had no intention of doing during this conference--public readings, writing competitions, clean up committee.

I found my friends and told them I had an 11:45 meeting with one of the literary agents. My friend Savannah looked at me from over the top rim of her glasses and said, "You are pitching to an agent?"

"Yes."

"Do you have a book in progress?"

"No."

"Lord have mercy, Keith," was the last thing she said about the meeting. My friends know enough to expect such things. Usually, they just shake their heads and hope not to be noticed talking to me towards the end of meetings and conferences, after my crazy has fully blossomed.

All through the first session of the day, I kept my panic level to a minimum. I began to think back on my training for interviews. I had developed an acceptable, if generic, "First Two Minutes" personal introduction in MBA school, however, that was ten years ago and was for use in business settings. I don't think a literary agent would care about my mastery of Excel spreadsheets or my award-winning accounting skills. Although, I could be wrong because I had never, EVER considered what an agent would want to hear or be looking for in a pitch from a potential author.

By the time my meeting with the agent had drawn nigh, I was sweaty and nervous. I had decided to definitely not mention Sh*t My Dad Says or other blogs/Twitter/Facebook-to-book successes. I also didn't want to say the name David Sedaris, the author-extraordinaire who every humor essay writer mentions when asked for comparison.

I scanned the files of my brain trying to remember some compliments people had relayed to me regarding my writing. After I discarded the compliments from my mother, I was left with three: (1) you are OK, (2) I like the way you write, and (3) you have a real talent for writing very self-deprecating humor without it being annoying at all. I decided I would go with number three.

I entered the room and firmly shook Ms. Rosenkranz's hand. Her firm shake and strong eye contact screamed, "I own my literary agency in New York." I was transfixed by her. I wanted to know all about her. Of course, had I either not been a slacker or researched who would be at the conference or listened to the conference lady when she asked me questions during registration, I would have probably gone to her business website and learned all I needed to know.

She had an egg timer on the table which was set for 15 minutes. She leaned forward in her chair to indicate how interested she was in hearing what I had to say, and asked, "So, what have you got for me?"

I immediately began rambling. Any training for a professional, well-groomed introduction I may have had in the past flew out the window of the Carnegie Center. I started by telling her I had a blog and loved it. I then moved on to how much I loved David Sedaris, and hoped to be able to someday publish a book similar to one of his. She nodded politely and told me that

Twitter/Facebook/Blog authors were rare, but it was certainly a remote possibility.

Then came the unmentionable. The moment in time that can never again be retrieved.

I had forgotten to tell her about the compliment I had previously received about my writing. I looked at the timer. I only had three minutes remaining, so I needed to move quickly. I immediately blurted out, *"I also would like to tell you that people have said I am great at self-defecating. But in a good way."*

The look on Ms. Rosenkranz's face briefly flashed to one of horror, but she quickly pulled herself back together, as only a New York literary agent can do, and smiled. She sat back in her chair and put down her ink pen. I knew something was wrong, but I wasn't sure what. I quickly retraced my verbal steps. I gasped out loud and covered my mouth when I realized what I had said to her. My eyes were wide with humiliation and my cheeks glowed. I was so stunned, I couldn't move or say anything. Thankfully, the timer bell rang, Ms. Rosenkranz jumped from her chair, headed to the door, and said, "Well, thank you for stopping by."

I staggered into the conference lobby and was asked by my friend how my meeting had gone. "I told her I literally shit on myself, but in a good way," I replied.

"Lord have mercy, Keith, let's just go to lunch," was all Savannah said as she held the door for me to exit the building.

In case you are wondering, I am currently still without agent representation.

Gun Control

Don't worry, dear readers. I am not going to get all
mavericky on you about guns. This isn't that kind of book. So you
will read neither "Guns don't kill people, people kill people," nor
"Shoot them all and let the Lord sort them out." Well, except for in
the previous sentence. That couldn't be helped. But that was the last
time, I promise.

In my limited experience, there is one particular group of
people I think should be restricted on gun usage and ownership. That
group is the elderly. Growing up in the hills of Eastern Kentucky,
most all of the men and women I knew packed heat. It was a way of
life. This included both my grandfather, Poppy Woodrow, and my
grandmother, Granny Mahala.

My family owned several different businesses in downtown
Hyden (Population 500) in the 1970's and 80's, and Poppy always
helped out with them. Mostly, he used the businesses as his home
base for his trading circle. Guns, knives, and government block
cheese were his three main inventory items, and he kept them tucked
away in a back room at Dad's store. I am not sure how many blocks
of commodity cheese a gun went for, but I can tell you that both our
family's refrigerator and the refrigerator of all my cousins' families
were always stocked with huge 10 pound blocks of creamy
processed government cheese. If you were never lucky enough to
taste a hunk of that cheese, then I pity you. It was delicious.

Poppy and his trading buddies liked to sit on the benches in
front of the town's courthouse and talk the day away. The talking
would eventually lead to the trading of stuff. Although they acted
like young boys needling and prodding one another over their items,
they were, let's face it, old men. Old men who sometimes got a little

carried away and careless. Such was the case the day Poppy brought one of his friends, Mr. Sizemore, into the store's back room, his office, to check out the gun Poppy had recently obtained with three knives and a block of cheese. No one was sure if the two men knew the gun was loaded or not, but what we do know is that as my Aunt Ruby tended the counter at Stewart's Entertainment Center, Poppy and Mr. Sizemore somehow unloaded the magazine of the pistol, shooting from the back room directly into the store showroom, totally destroying one Pioneer Home Stereo System and one front window. Aunt Ruby was stunned silent, then checked herself for shot marks. Seeing none and thinking she was being robbed, she began telephoning my father for help. Poppy and Mr. Sizemore suddenly appeared, leaving the back room as if nothing had happened. Mr. Sizemore was carrying the pistol that still stank of fresh shot while Poppy handed Aunt Ruby two fresh blocks of cheese and attached his newly traded for pocket watch to his belt.

Woodrow's bride, my granny Mahala, was no better. Granny was a typical Appalachian woman who always wore a house dress, sensible shoes, and never moved at a fast pace. She always kept a loaded pistol in her purse. Always. Anytime she was riding in a car with anyone in the family (she didn't drive), and the car was stopped by the police, be it for speeding or a standard roadside-block that was common in the 1980's, the family member who was driving would sweat bullets until they were released by the police because Granny was sitting as the co-pilot with loaded heat in her purse.

She was also very protective over her pistol purse. If she was going to leave it at home for any reason, she would hide it. One particular time, she hid it in the washing machine. The next day, she decided to wash her kitchen rugs. She threw the rugs in the machine, set it to wash, and thankfully, left the laundry room and went into the living room to watch her stories on television. What happened next is what one would imagine happening if you had to shoot your way out of a washing machine. Granny had forgotten about her purse, complete with the loaded gun in it, when she loaded the washing machine and turned it on. The jarring from the machine set off the pistol several times, leaving holes in the washer, dryer, wall and window. Remarkably, Granny was not hurt, but was upset she had to miss the second half of *The Young and the Restless* that day.

So you can see why my concern for gun control really centers on the older population. In fact, my Dad has a gun safe, and I am considering changing the lock on it and keeping the key when he turns 75. After all, he is a direct descendent of Poppy and Granny. What chance at all does he have?

Go Tell It on the Mountain

Growing up, I was an oddity—a kid who lived within the city limits of our county seat, Hyden, population 500. Tell anyone you are from southeastern Kentucky, and visions of nearly impenetrable hills, heavy forests, and secluded communities immediately come to mind. And for the majority of people I knew during my childhood, this was a true description of their home. They lived in the rugged hollows and valleys carved into the ancient Appalachian Mountains that dominate the landscape of Leslie County. I, however, did not.

I learned to ride my Huffy Avenger bicycle in the gridlock of traffic borne from Hyden's multitude of smoothly paved city streets, including one three-way intersection with a working traffic signal that could be set to turn red, yellow, and green—although it was almost always left flashing yellow in all directions. I lived on Hickory Street, surrounded by neighbors, all with matching small, tidy lawns. The water I drank was from a city water filtration system. We had no need for such peculiarities as septic tanks or satellite television dishes.

My friends who lived outside the city limits, though, had it rough. Their parents rallied political leaders in hopes of having the dirt roads leading to their homes leveled, graveled, and, if a particularly good favor was owed or political scandal known, perhaps paved. In winter, they often were stuck in their mountain home for weeks at a time due to even the smallest amount of snow. There were no plows or city services outside the limits. On the other hand, I complained when city services cleared the streets in winter, preventing me from sledding down the clean concrete of Hospital Hill.

I knew Appalachia was famous for its old-fashioned, come-before-lunch-stay-until-after-dinner, sing-and-make-a-lot-of-noise, catch-the-Holy-Ghost type of religion, but I never experienced it. In town, you were either Baptist or Presbyterian. Being raised on the north side of Hyden, I was Presbyterian. To get to my church, I walked a hundred feet down the nice sidewalk from my house. I put in my allotted hour for praise then raced my sister back down the street to our house where Sunday dinner would be served. Our Presbyterian services were dignified, ritual-filled, and stuffy. The singing was horrible, but the timing was exact. Anything over an hour was unacceptable and caused more than one indignant throat-clearing and check-of-the-watch by impatient parishioners. I often wondered as we were sitting down to our post-worship dinner, if someone in Greasy Creek or Cutshin or other rural outpost in the county was at that very moment still in church tossing a snake and/or burning coal around the sanctuary. I had heard about places of worship called Holiness, Pentecostal, and Church of God from friends at school and from a few cousins whose errant parents had strayed from the Presbyterian fold. However, I was kept sheltered from this strange way of churching by the mere sophistication of the city of Hyden and the Elders of Central Presbyterian, also known as The Frozen Chosen, due to the lack of any emotions shown during services. Knowing these forbidden churches were just a few mere miles from me and that I could never see what happened during their worship made them all the more exotic and alluring to me.

By the time I graduated college, I was ready to move on from Kentucky. The mountains that had always protected and given me comfort began to grip too tightly and to block my evolving world view. Even though there were many advantageous differences living in town, the Appalachian culture was primarily the same no matter where you lived–Hickory Street, up Rockhouse Creek or over on Hell-Fer-Certain. New ideas and liberal thinking was shunned more often than not in favor of traditional values and generation-old ways of doing things. This conservatism began to smother me as much as the very mountains themselves.

I spread my wings and landed in Florida. I soon began the ritual of most college graduates in their first career jobs—working ten to twelve hours a day trying to impress your boss and get a promotion that would no longer place you at the bottom of the company totem pole. But, possibly more importantly, I worked hard to be a success for the people in my hometown. Appalachian communities are so close and tightly-woven that when one of the children leaves the area, everyone knows. Once gone, children of Appalachia remain very much in the fold of those left behind in their hometowns. Any achievement, big or small, by the mountain refugee is celebrated as a victory for the community. It is as if the town has sent someone out beyond the borders of its ridges and peaks to prove to the rest of the world that we can do anything they can do. The community says, "We may be hillbillies, but we are just as competent as you flatlanders. Just look at what we can do."

While striving for this goal of recognition, however, I was saddled with the shame of trying to distance myself from my Appalachian roots. I felt if others heard my accent and my drawl, they would automatically assume I was not intelligent. If they knew where I was from, they would only associate me with moonshiners and the movie "Deliverance." Because of that, I never ate soup beans and cornbread in public or spoke of my hometown's annual Coon on the Log contest held every fourth of July at the Fish and Game Center. Instead, when asked I would simply say I was from Kentucky. For residents of Florida—most of whom are not at all Southern by any means other than geography—all states south of Ohio and Pennsylvania and east of Oklahoma are considered The South and bunched indiscriminately as one, so they asked no further questions about my Kentucky heritage. My fictional sophistication made me think very highly of myself, and get totally and completely above my raising.

It was during this time of self-discovery that I received a phone call from my mother telling me I needed to come home to Kentucky for a family funeral. My sister's father-in-law had passed away unexpectedly. I tried to protest, saying it wasn't *really* a family funeral since it was just my sister's in-law, but in Appalachia, entire families marry each other. Her husband's family was now mine. Respect for the dead must now be shown no matter how far you have to travel to do it. I knew there was no use in arguing the point further when my mother started using both my first and middle names. Neither time nor distance can stop a southern boy from crumbling with fear when his mother uses his middle name in anger. Once I heard, "Keith Allen, I don't care how busy you think you are, you will book the next flight to Lexington and have your rear end at this house by no later than the day after tomorrow," I knew I was heading home.

Over the next day and a half in further talks with family members, I discovered the funeral was to be held out in the county at one of those mysterious, exotic churches I always had heard so much about, but never been allowed inside. Oh sure, it was only a Methodist church, but it was still *out in the county,* and one could always hope for a wayward snake to slither inside or the Holy Ghost to goose a lady while she mourned. At the very least, I hoped to see someone anoint something with oil.

The day of the funeral was unusually warm for February in southeastern Kentucky. The temperature soared into the upper seventies by mid-morning. I began to wonder if I had made a mistake by bringing a heavy suit to wear instead of a lightweight one more suitable for the heat of Florida, but the heavier one was a designer brand, making it a much better choice for my grand reappearance as a hometown-boy-made-good. I could only hope the Lower Bowen's Creek Methodist Church had a central cooling system.

As I came out of my childhood bedroom at my parent's home, I noticed my father ready to go. He was looking miserable, dressed in his best black suit, but my mother was still in her housecoat. Conveniently, she had volunteered to babysit my sister's three-year-old twins, so Sis would not have to deal with their rambunctiousness in a crowded church. My mother has always had a knack of slyly convincing the rest of the family, particularly my sister and me, to do her bidding without realizing we are doing it. One minute we would be playing badminton in the backyard and the next we would be in the kitchen washing the dishes from dinner while my mother was resting in her chair watching "M*A*S*H," neither of us knowing how exactly we got there. The irony of insisting I travel over eight hundred miles for this funeral while she stayed at home in her housecoat, though, was not lost on Mom. She busied herself with pacifiers and sippy cups to avoid any eye contact with me until my father and I headed out in his four-wheel drive SUV for the trip to Lower Bowen's Creek.

By the time we finally arrived at the church in the nether regions of the county, I was both carsick and grateful we were in a four-wheel drive. We hopped out of the car, and immediately I noticed how hot it had gotten. The sun was working overtime this mid-winter's day and the temperature had increased to over eighty degrees, hotter here than in Florida. We walked inside the small church to find it filled-to-near capacity and the inside temperature even hotter than the outside. I immediately began sweating from every pore. I noticed most people there were wearing short-sleeved shirts and slacks or even t-shirts and jeans. I cursed my vanity that insisted I wear my designer suit, but told myself it would be worth it if only for the purpose of demonstrating my success to all who saw me.

We found a seat near the front of the sanctuary and sat down. I spotted my sister sitting with her husband's family on the opposite side of the church, near the front. She seemed to be frantically waving away a bug. I then noticed a lot of people in attendance swatting away flying objects and ducking their heads to avoid being hit by incoming insects. I looked up and noticed in the very top of the church, where the two sides of the roof meet forming the apex, was a hornet's nest. All the activity and out-of-season heat in the church must have roused them from their winter slumber. I kept a leery eye on the nest, but thought, "What is the worst that can happen? We are in a church, for heaven's sake."

As the service began, everyone forgot about the insects and focused on the activities up front. Everyone, I should say, except my father. As the eulogy was read by a grieving family member, an overly-zealous hornet started buzzing around him, and he was acting as if it were the most dangerous thing in the world. I ignored him completely, appalled by his actions. This was my debut to the folks back home as a sophisticated modern man. "We are from TOWN. Have some manners, old man," I thought to myself. I also wondered if at that very moment Mother was having another cup of coffee and reading her Stephen King book while the twins napped.

As the preacher began a solemn sermon—not the Hellfire and brimstone I had hoped for in a mountain church funeral—Dad's nemesis began to get crazed from all the swipes he had swung at it. The hornet was mad and began to get aggressive and fight back. After a few more futile swats with his hand, Dad, sweating as if he'd been working in the fields, leaned over to me and said, "Gimme something to kill that thing with." I was, of course, horrified.

"We are in a church," I whispered.

"I said gimme something to kill that thing with."

"No. Dad. We. Are. In. A. Church. We can't kill anything in a church."

"If we don't kill it, it is going to sting us!" Dad was now visibly shaken at the thought of being stung, sweating profusely, and speaking well above a whisper.

"If we do kill it, we will go to Hell, because WE ARE IN A CHURCH," was my final rebuttal. At this point, I noticed a couple of people disapprovingly glance over at us from other pews. I decided it was up to me to maintain some sort of dignity and grace for our family's namesake and for my homecoming. I was no longer a local yokel. I had moved on and up. I was a successful businessman who lived in the city and who was raised in town. I simply refused to be the local boy who was now a big city success only to show up at the Lower Bowen's Creek Methodist Church and cause a scene at a funeral.

I evoked my philosophy for most all life situations: ignore it and it will go away. I kept thinking if I didn't further respond to Dad's comments or requests for "something to kill that thing with," he would let it go. I built an imaginary brick wall between us. He couldn't see me, and I couldn't see him. I crossed my legs, wiped the sweat from my forehead, and began nodding at the pastor as if I had been listening to his sermon this entire time.

In my peripheral vision, I saw Dad eyeing the Bible sitting in its holder on the back of the pew in front of us. He had a hint of recognition in his face. Had he been a cartoon character, a light bulb would have illuminated above his head. As he glimpsed over at me, I immediately began tearing down the brick wall I had just built. I frantically shook my head no. "Surely to God, you aren't thinking of…" was all I had time to whisper before Dad reached and grabbed the Bible.

I watched in horror as my father, with an ever so small smile on his face, tracked the hornet with his eyes. He was a hunter stalking his prey. The pastor was just finishing up his sermon as the hornet finally lit on the window right beside Dad. He then very carefully took the Bible, and in slow motion so as not to scare the bug, forcefully pressed the book flat against the window. The preacher finished his sermon with, "Let us pray."

In the silence between the pastor's words and the prayer, I heard the crunch of every little hornet bone being crushed by God's holy word. I could almost see the angels crying above us. If ever the Holy Ghost were going to enter a physical form, it would be now. It would enter the body of that lowly hornet and have it come back to life and sting the hell out of us both. But instead of that, God chose another form of revenge, one that, really, should be expected when you purposefully plan and execute a murder inside the sanctuary of a church, even if it is Methodist. After the "crunch" of the hornet, we both heard a "clink" of glass. We looked at the window and realized that the pressure of the attack had knocked the glass loose from the window pane. All that was now holding the sheet of glass in place inside the pane was the hornet carcass and my father's Bible pressed against it.

I was stunned. I said a quick, futile prayer that Dad would continue his current pose and hold the glass in place for the remainder of the service, if not until everyone had vacated the church. But Dad accepted our fate and removed his hold on the window. The glass immediately fell about two inches to the stone window ledge and shattered making such a loud noise people all up and down Lower Bowen's Creek could hear it. Certainly, the hundred or so people inside the church did. I sat still, afraid to move, afraid to blink. Dad acted as if nothing out of the ordinary had happened, and simply wiped the bug guts off the Bible and slowly returned it to the back of the pew in front of us.

Instead of having live music or a real person sing at the funeral, the family chose to pay tribute to the deceased by playing his favorite song via a boom box placed on the podium. The pastor, trying to ignore the fact that someone had just shattered a window in his church, hit the play button and the first strands of a guitar solo began streaming out of the speakers. At first I thought I was mistaken, but within a couple of seconds there was no doubt about it. We were listening to Lynyrd Skynyrd's "Freebird." Dad and I both stared forward towards the podium as if the Southern Rock band were there in the flesh. As we watched the boom box with great interest and concern, we acted as if we had no idea why everyone in the church was staring at us. Eventually, I sneaked a glance up and over at my sister who had turned her entire body around in her pew and was staring at us open mouthed with a dumbfounded look on her face. I quickly averted my eyes.

I told myself I could make it through this debacle. I had worked so hard at becoming suave and citified, but it was at this very moment I realized it had all been a sham. I was no better than any of these people. In fact, they were much classier and gracious than I could ever be. Here I was in a sweaty overpriced suit with my father, the insect murderer, inside a church listening to "Freebird" being played from a cassette in a boom box at a funeral. I then began to feel the first tingling of laughter building inside me. I glanced over at my father who was looking at me with eyes that were begging to laugh. That was all it took to burst the dam. I started laughing uncontrollably, shaking all over, which in turn was all it took for my father to start in as well. We both not only laughed, but guffawed, cried, and gasped while the crowd tried to ignore us and continue their dignified grieving.

After the ceremony, we kept our heads down, made no eye contact with anyone, and headed straight for the car. We wanted to get out of Lower Bowen's Creek before people could find out the names of the two uncivilized men who broke their window and acted like heathens, but my sister stepped in front of us, blocking our path. She immediately let us know that she had informed the Deacon we would be sending a check to pay for a new church window, which in turn started us laughing all over again. She left us trying to control ourselves, drying our eyes, and starting our long way back to the big, sophisticated, city of Hyden.

The Blitz - How One Play Changed My Football Career

I have only played one football game my entire life, Pledge Bowl, my freshman year of college. For some unknown reason, the Greek community at Transylvania University (I promise it's a real school) thought it would be swell if the freshman pledges to each fraternity played each other in a football playoff-type tournament every year. This was a big deal to the members of Phi Kappa Tau, my fraternity. It was our first chance as newbies to prove our loyalty to the Greek letters we proudly wore on our chests.

I was reluctant to play, and voiced my concerns to anyone who would listen that I had no experience playing football and didn't even know the rules. The fraternity was adamant I not sit out, but no one ever explained to me what to do or how to do it. Perhaps they thought the ability to play this game was inherently found in the genetic makeup of male DNA. They were wrong. All I knew about football was to be tough and mean, talk smack, and occasionally pat my teammates on the rear.

The morning of the Pledge Bowl was a brisk, fall morning. The trees on campus were bursting with color, the sun was shining, and there was the scent of autumn in the air. Everyone seemed pumped and ready for action. Everyone except me. I had a deer-in-headlights look and an upset stomach. I didn't know how I was going to pull this off. Finally seeing me in my near- panicked frenzy, a couple of the upperclassmen brothers, Chip and Jay, took me aside. They said, "We understand what you're going through. The best thing to help is this," holding up a bottle of bourbon and two shot glasses.

At that point in my eighteen-year-old life, wine coolers and an occasional beer was all the alcohol I had drunk, but the brothers seemed to be sincere, so I took them up on their offer and downed two quick hits of Makers Mark. As the liquor warmed my insides, it numbed the negative thoughts in my head. I didn't care if I knew the rules or not, I was going to win this Pledge Bowl for my fraternity! Roll Tau Roll! Bring on those Pi Kappa Alphas!

Our team started the game playing defense. As we lined up on the field against Pi Kappa Alpha, everyone looked serious. Game faces were on, except mine. I had my big grin face on. And a case of the giggles. I then decided to talk some smack.

"Hey Pikes, I bet you throw like girls. Hey Pikes, today I am giving out free lollipops and whoop ass, and I'm all out of lollipops," I yelled to the other team inches from my face waiting for the ball to be snapped into play. Since no one had seen me downing the whiskey shots, my teammates looked at me with confusion and most of the Pikes were equally stunned. When the ball was hiked to the quarterback, I just started running for any player on the other team. As I ran, I let out a primal scream that sounded like I had been speared by a hot poker.

In my defense, no one ever explained to me that there was a difference in flag football and regular football. Had someone said, "The reason we are wearing these long, flowing streamers out of our shorts is that in order to tackle someone, you simply grab his streamer," I would have done that very thing. But, no one had explained that to me. In my bourbon-fueled rage, I rammed into an unassuming Pike pledge who was watching his quarterback try to find someone to throw the ball to downfield, and tackled him with all the force and grit I had in me. We were both airborne for a few seconds then landed on the ground and rolled three full rotations before coming to a stop, my scream the only noise on the entire field.

I stood up and looked around, proud of what I had just done. The poor guy I tackled was crumpled on the field, trying to regain his breath. The two referees pulled their yellow streamers out and threw them into the air. I didn't know what that meant, so I pulled my streamers out of my shorts, threw them into the mix, and for good measure, patted one of the refs on the butt. A bit of a skirmish between the teams ensued and was quickly broken up by college administrators. I was still oblivious to the fact this was all due to me and my actions. It was then made clear to me by one of the referees that I was being thrown out of not only the game, but the entire Pledge Bowl.

I can't say that I wasn't happy with the news my football debut was over after only one play. I was, however, bewildered with the reasoning behind the decision. I kept telling my brothers I had told them I didn't know how to play, but they just kept laughing, patting me on the back, and telling me that I was a legend in the making. Having been banned from the game itself, I found Chip and Jay, and proceeded to sip bourbon and watch my brothers play from the sidelines. It is probably no coincidence I ended my college experience as president of the fraternity.

In the years following that historic day in college, I have continued my friendship with these same men. Our love for each other now extends to wives and partners, children, and even a grandchild or two. I owe this circle to the sport of football. Even if I still can't tell the difference from a fullback and a halfback, I can still be found on crisp, fall afternoons, sitting at some tailgate with my brothers, sipping on bourbon.

The first question often asked after mentioning a sporting event is "Who won?" But sports are so much more than a competition where one wins and the other loses. Sports give grown men the chance to paint their faces and wear horns or cheese or clown wigs on their heads in public without ridicule. They offer us a way to connect not only with teammates and opponents, but to magically bond with thirty thousand people all wearing the same color and yelling the same chant. The true benefit of any sport, whether it be a small college football pledge bowl, the NCAA Final Four basketball tournament, or a t-ball game at the local park, is the relationships forged that stay with you the rest of your life. Because there is nothing like being with an old friend and hearing the words, "Remember that time…"

Pump #5

My world in the spring of 1989 was a beautifully wild tiger just waking up, and I had that cat's tail firmly in my grip. I was one month away from graduating Leslie County High School, and finally being freed from the intense scrutiny that can only be experienced by growing up the son of the mayor in an Appalachian Kentucky community with a population less than 1,000 people.

I was a good kid. I did and said all the correct things required of good kids. I was never in trouble with my parents. I came home as my curfew alarm began chiming. I studied and made good grades. I volunteered at my church and in my community. However, even though I was legally an adult—I had recently celebrated my eighteenth birthday—I still was subject to the "as-long-as-you-live-under-our-roof-you-are-a-child" rule of parenting, which to a responsible young man such as myself seemed unfair. So, when my friend Grace told me the band Bon Jovi, the greatest band of the 1980s, was performing a concert in nearby Lexington on a Sunday—meaning a school night—I just assumed my parents would never allow me to go.

Imagine my great surprise when my parents were not only agreeable, but also told me I was becoming a responsible young adult, and it was time they let me have some freedoms. Then in an unexpected show of confidence, my father said I should drive his new Nissan Pathfinder SUV to the concert. He was concerned my 1978 Nissan Stanza that barely made it back and forth the two miles to school each day, and had only one working windshield wiper, would not handle a trip to Lexington, especially if it rained since the working wiper was on the passenger side.

The evening of the concert, as I was putting the final touches on my Bon Jovi mix tape for the road trip, my mother extended another gift of maturity to me. She gave me her BP gas credit card. Until this point in my life, my gas purchases had consisted of spending, at most, five dollars at each visit to a gas station. Most of the time, I put in the tank the amount of the spare change I had in the car console and my jeans pockets. To fill up a tank completely and then pay with plastic was unheard of in my group of high school friends. Suddenly, I was a man. A man who was responsible enough to drive his father's new SUV and use his mother's gas station credit card. A man who filled his gas tank to the brim.

I called my friend Grace, who was going to the concert with me, told her I would pick her up after I filled the Pathfinder with gas at the BP Mart, and let her know we would be riding in style. I also told her the Pathfinder had a state of the art cassette system, so not only would we not have to listen to AM radio as we usually did in my car, but I also had made a totally awesome mix-tape of nothing but Bon Jovi songs for the trip. She said her older cousin had given her two Bartles & Jaymes wine coolers for the evening, and we would drink them before going into the arena. Our adult evening of rocking and rolling was all set.

My hometown of Hyden was, and still is, a beautiful mountain village resembling something Normal Rockwell would have painted. The new BP Mart built on the edge of town broke that mold. It was modern. The store was covered in bright lights and neon. It had multiple pumps, and you pumped the gas yourself, which was a first in Hyden. There was a nice, well-stocked store with automatic doors. Once inside, there were shelves full of snacks, coolers of drinks, and an entire counter for lottery tickets. It had quickly become the northwest anchor of the teenager-cruising strip in Hyden, so it was always a social trip when I went to BP.

I proudly entered the station island, feeling like an adult— an adult with a credit card—who fully intended to fill his tank to the brim with gasoline. I pulled in beside Pump #5, and for the first time in my young life, clicked the handle of the pump to automatically fill up. While the gas was flowing, I decided to go inside for some tasty treats for the road, and more importantly, to see if anyone I knew was there so I could brag about going to see Bon Jovi live in concert on a school night.

I chatted with a few people, bought some chips and soda, and paid for everything with the BP credit card. It was quite a rush. I wondered if my mother felt this same power fill her veins when she paid with the card.

I now just had to pick up my friend Grace and then we were Lexington bound. I couldn't stop thinking about what a huge night this was for me, and that all my hard work trying to be a responsible person had really paid off. I hopped into Dad's Pathfinder and shifted the gear into "drive." I then pumped the gas pedal.

Nothing.

I checked to make sure I actually had turned the key and started the car before again trying the gas pedal.

I had.

I checked to make sure I was in Drive and not Neutral.

I was.

I pumped the gas pedal harder. "RRRRRRRRREEEEEEERRRRRR" went the car. My RPM-monitor was off the hook. I thought to myself, "Gee, even my Stanza has more power than this Pathfinder." Suddenly, my back was pasted to the seat of the car as the SUV blasted off and I heard a horrible noise that sounded like metal being pulled over concrete. I quickly slammed on my brakes and looked into my rear view mirror. I will never forget what I saw reflected behind me.

In my hurried and distracted state, I had forgotten to take the gas pump nozzle out of the Pathfinder. Not only had I pulled the gas hose off, but I actually had pulled the entire gas pump out of the ground. I sat there, in complete horror, watching gas spew out of the hole where the pump had been minutes earlier. The gas was arcing in the air like a small geyser, landing directly on the trunk of a BMW whose owner stood gap-mouthed with her own gas nozzle in hand.

My knees were wobbly, and my eyes were full of tears. I couldn't catch my breath. My immediate thought was that if I just kept driving the gas pump would eventually fall away from the car, hopefully, before I got to the first toll booth on the Daniel Boone Parkway, the road that lead out of town. But, being from a town the size of Hyden, there would be no denying who had done this horrible thing. "Perhaps, no one noticed," I mumbled to myself. "Yes, no one noticed, let's go with that. It probably didn't sound as loud as I thought it did."

I placed the car in park and eased out of the vehicle. The front of the convenience store was all windows, and at this point they were completely filled by people staring outside at the scene in front of them. Correction: they all were staring except one boy who had his arms wrapped around himself and was doubled over from maniacal laughter.

Great.

It was Caleb, a guy I only sort of knew from school. Now he had witnessed my greatest blunder. For a brief moment, the horror of what had just happened actually disappeared and all I could see was Caleb laughing at me. My only thought was whether I could somehow convince him not to say anything about this to anyone at school. A piece of metal from the gas pump came unhinged and fell to the ground with a clanging noise, finally snapping me back to reality. I took a deep breath and walked into the store.

The crowd divided as if I were Moses parting the Red Sea, giving me a wide berth to the store clerk. I thought if I acted as if I ripped down gas pumps every day no one would really notice what was happening. So with my poker face, I nonchalantly said, "Yeah, I have had a little problem out on pump #5."

The clerk looked at me with fear and shock in her eyes and simply said, "Honey, you sure have." I then asked to use the telephone. She placed the phone on the counter, and I dialed home while she went to the back of the store to hit the "Emergency Shut-Off Gas" button.

In all my 18 years, I never had known my father to answer a telephone. He would sit in his chair beside the phone while my mother was outside working in her flowers, and he would let it just ring or yell outside to her that it was ringing before he would answer it. On this particular occasion, however, Dad decided to change his ways. The phone was no longer something he feared. He would start answering it. In fact, he would start right at that very moment.

Super.

"Hello?" he said, as if he answered phones daily.

"Hey, Dad! Um, I am out here at the BP Mart, and, well, I have had a problem. It appears that I forgot to take the nozzle out of the Pathfinder after filling it up with gas, and I pulled out with it still attached, and I have ripped the gas pump out of the ground," I cheerfully said, hoping by keeping my tone light and airy he would think it funny.

"Damn, Keith," was his response. That was it—just "Damn, Keith."

Then I heard a click. He hung up. He had hung up on me! He was not going to tell my mother, and they were not going to come help me. What in Heaven's name was I going to do now? I then noticed that the crowd of people in the store was still watching me, hanging on my every word. Again, trying to appear calm, cool, and collected, I pretended my father was still on the phone talking to me. I answered fake questions, shook my head, and pretended to listen closely before responding, "No, it is still attached to the car...I dragged it about ten feet away...No, I don't think there is much damage, well, at least not to the Pathfinder." I was forced to stop when the "EEH EEH EEH" alarm that a landline phone makes when you leave it off the hook too long started. In the quiet of the shocked crowd, the noise from the phone alarm could be heard all over the store. I was not fazed, however. I could not let on that no one was coming to help. "Okay," I said, "see you in just a bit then," having to speak loudly over the blaring alarm. I handed back the "EEH EEH EEH-ING" phone receiver to the store clerk, who had returned from shutting down all gas flow to the station. I stood there looking around. The crowd of people stood there looking at me. The clerk was busy calling the owner of the station, the insurance company, the Department of Transportation, the police, and I suspect the local newspaper reporter. "My folks are coming," I assured the crowd. Secretly, I was contemplating how far I could run before the police or an angry mob could catch me.

My dad owned a stereo store and movie rental business called Stewart's Entertainment Center. He had bought an old-time milk delivery van to use as his stereo delivery vehicle. It looked like a bread delivery truck, but a mini-sized version. It was short, squat, and perfectly square. It only had a driver's seat, and Dad used a milk crate for a passenger to sit on as the co-pilot. Along with no actual seat, there was also no door on the passenger side. He had struck a deal with a guy in town who painted cars to trade a stereo system for a custom paint job for the van. The painter in return for his stereo had outdone himself and had painted the van in a purple, pink, and violet tie-dye motif. He had also painted dancing California raisins, a popular cartoon during the eighties, all over the wagon. In musical shaped letters the sides and back of the van read "Raisin' Ruckus, Stewart's Entertainment Center."

Just as I had given up all hope and was getting ready to make a break for it from the gas station, I saw a purple haze on the horizon. Thankfully, most of the crowd had stopped staring at me and were now outside gathered around the hole where the gas pump used to be. As the purple haze came closer and developed into a solid image, I was horrified.

Please no.

The loud rumbling noise confirmed it.

God no.

The Raisin' Ruckus Van then came into view, puttering down the street, my mom sitting on the milk crate, jiggling along, and Dad flooring it to its max speed of twenty miles per hour. "Why, oh why, did they drive the Raisin' Ruckus Van?! They could have driven anything but the Raisin' Ruckus Van!" I said to no one in particular.

As the crowd saw the Purple Wagon pull into the station, they looked at it and then at me. It made sense, really. I mean, what would you expect the parents of someone who just ripped a gas pump out of the ground to drive? A purple tie-dyed Raisin' Ruckus van seemed appropriate.

They came to a stop, the van's engine loudly backfired, and they got out, Dad slamming his door, Mom sliding off her milk crate.

Dad immediately passed by me to go check on his Pathfinder. Mom walked up to me and stared. I could tell the crowd was listening; the air was ripe with anticipation of what she would say to me. Finally, she yelled, "Keith Allen, people tell me that you are smart, your test scores say that you are smart, your grades indicate that you are smart, but you SURE AS HELL DON'T ACT IT!" She then went to check on the Pathfinder, and my father's state of mind. I also heard her ask the local policeman on the scene if I could be arrested for this. I think she was hoping for an affirmative answer.

Eventually, the drama was over. I had filled out all the proper paperwork, given official statements, and even posed by the hole in the ground for the local newspaper reporter to get a photo. The gas station was shut down for the day. The police left, and the crowd dispersed. The only damage to the Pathfinder was that the gas funnel had been slightly pulled out of place. Being an idiotic, irresponsible 18-year-old boy who was in no way a responsible adult, I stood in front of my parents and asked, "So, should I go on home or to the concert?"

My dad just looked at me in disgust and walked back to the Purple Wagon. Mom said, "I think if you were to go home right now, your father may actually kill you, so just go on to the concert."

After I picked up my friend Grace and explained why I was so late, she was stunned, but not mad. She decided to drive and let me have both wine coolers to calm my nerves. We made it to the concert, and although we missed the opening act, Bon Jovi rocked the house. I admit, though, I did not enjoy it as much as I thought I would.

I lived through the humiliation that followed. As I feared, Caleb told everyone at school what he witnessed, and I was voted "Most Likely to Work at a Gas Station" by my senior class. Later that summer, I had a part-time job with a local attorney, mainly to earn enough money to pay the BP Mart's insurance deductible for the repairs. I was also working hard at reestablishing my reputation as a responsible person to my parents, and trying to prove they had not, despite what my father kept insisting, raised a complete lunatic.

One day at work, after delivering some legal papers to the courthouse in the next town over from mine, I realized my car needed gas. Without noticing the name of the station, I pulled into the Hazard BP Mart. My mother had immediately taken the credit card from me after "the incident," so I was back to putting small amounts of gas in the vehicle. After putting in ten- dollars-worth of gas, I triple checked that the hose was safely back in its holder on the pump and nowhere near my car, and walked inside to write a check for my purchase. When the clerk saw my name and address on the check, she looked up and said that she would need to clear this with the manager. I assumed she meant she would need approval because it was an out-of-town check. The manager joined her in the corner and I overheard arguing about who would ask me. Finally, the manager walked over and said, "We were just wondering if you are the same Keith Stewart from Hyden that ripped down the gas pump in our Hyden store?" Humiliated, I nodded an affirmative, turned, and hurried out the door.

As I made my way back to the car, I noticed the manager had followed me outside and was pretending to check the trash cans sitting beside each gas pump. It was obvious he had come out to make sure I had not left the hose attached to my car. "I double checked it. There is no need to worry," I said.

"Hey man, no problem. I just don't want the same thing happening here. Listen, if you want, next time you are here, just come in first and let me know, and I'll pump the gas for you. I don't mind at all." I forced a smile, revved up my Nissan and pulled out, clenching my butt cheeks and holding my breath as I pulled away from the island, hoping not to hear metal against concrete.

Acknowledgements

I would like to thank and acknowledge the following for their support: Andy, Mom, Dad, & Sis, who continually allow me to write and post intimate details of their lives without (too much) grief; Kate Larken, Anne Shelby, and Silas House, who were kind, welcoming, and supportive to an unemployed CPA who showed up at a workshop wanting to seriously write about funny things; Donna and Trish, without the two of you, life would not be nearly as fun; Savannah, Jay, and Staci, my unofficial writing/therapy group; Becky, who tirelessly read and edited even when she didn't want to; my Appalachian Writers Workshop family in Hindman, KY, you are the best of the best; the Southampton Writers Conference at Stonybrook University, especially the tutelage of Patricia Marx; the Mountain Heritage Literary Festival at Lincoln Memorial University, for making me say, "I am a writer!" over and over; the Erma Bombeck Humor Writers Conference for introducing me to HumorOutcasts.com; KY Story Press, The Good Men Project, and Humoroutcasts.com for previously publishing some of the essays in the book; Donna Cavanagh, who gave me the chance and opportunity to start this book, and the encouragement to finish it; and finally, all the readers of my blog, astrongmanscupoftea.com, without you, I would never have continued chronicling my embarrassing life.

About the Author:

Keith Stewart's strange adventures usually occur near his Appalachian hometown of Hyden, Kentucky, although he can be just as easily found wandering the streets of nearby Lexington at any given moment. Before he shed his corporate identity, he worked as a certified public accountant for a multi-national company. He now enjoys less stressful work with much less pay, blogs at www.astrongmanscupoftea.com, and is as happy as a clam with his husband Andy, and their two dogs, Duke and Dudley. He has been nominated for the Pushcart Prize, and been published in several anthologies, Kudzu, and Pine Mountain Sand and Gravel. He is contributor for HumorOutcasts.com and the GoodMedProject.com.

Made in the USA
Lexington, KY
12 April 2016